Chag S

Open this book and
inspire
ignite Je
teach a lesson or two
enlight and discover
take it all in - from cover to cover.
As you enjoy the Chag from beginning to end
And spend time with family and friends
Remember your Oorah family who cares
And will keep in touch throughout the whole year.

- Rabbi Chaim Mintz

732-730-1000 · OORAH.ORG · THEZONE.ORG · TORAHMATES.ORG · JEWISHLITTLESTAR.ORG

THE LURIE EDITION

וידעת היום

Now I Know

לא תרצח
לא תנאף
לא תגנב
לא תענה
לא תחמד

אנכי ה'
לא יהיה
לא תשא
זכור את
כבד את

Emunah: Turning Belief into Knowledge

RABBI AVROHOM KATZ

וידעת היום
Now

THE LURIE EDITION

I KNOW

Emunah: Turning Belief into Knowledge

RABBI AVROHOM KATZ

Copyright © 2019 by Rabbi Avrohom Katz

ISBN 978-1-60091-655-7
All rights reserved. No part of this book may be reproduced or transmitted in any form or by any means (electronic, photocopying, recording or otherwise) without prior permission of the publisher.

Distributed by:
Israel Bookshop Publications
501 Prospect Street
Lakewood, NJ 08701
Tel: (732) 901-3009 / Fax: (732) 901-4012
www.israelbookshoppublications.com
info@israelbookshoppublications.com

Printed in the United States of America

Distributed in Israel by:
Tfutza Publications
P.O.B. 50036
Beitar Illit 90500
972-2-650-9400

Distributed in Europe by:
Lehmanns
Unit E Viking Industrial Park
Rolling Mill Road,
Jarrow, Tyne & Wear NE32 3DP
44-191-430-0333

Distributed in Australia by:
Gold's Book and Gift Company
3-13 William Street
Balaclava 3183
613-9527-8775

Distributed in South Africa by:
Kollel Bookshop
Northfield Centre
17 Northfield Avenue
Glenhazel 2192
27-11-440-6679

DEDICATION

With tremendous gratitude to a special friend, a stalwart of the Newcastle Jewish community and a generous supporter of many worthy causes both in Gateshead and Newcastle

Mr. Geoffrey Lurie ה׳ ישמרהו ויחייהו

who, with characteristic warm-heartedness and enthusiasm for Torah values, has sponsored the publication of this book.

In memory of his father

Aaron Lurie

אהרן בן יחיאל ע״ה

נפטר יב׳ שבט תשי״א

January 18, 1951

His mother

Ethel Lurie

עטיל בת אליעזר אהרן ע״ה

נפטרה ג׳ אדר שני תשל״ט

March 2, 1979

His sister

Beulah Benjamin (Lurie)

ביילא בת אהרן ע״ה

נפטרה יב׳ אלול תשע״ח

August 23, 2018

In the merit of this great mitzvah, may Hakadosh Baruch Hu bless him, together with all his family, with good health and happiness, *brachah v'hatzlachah ad mei'ah v'esrim shanah.*

בס"ד

חודש סיון תשע"ח לפ"ק

הנה קבלתי עלים לתרופה מידידי אהובי עוז מגדולי מזכי הרבים באנגליה הרב ר' אברהם כהן כ"ץ שליט"א אשר נתקשרתי עמו בעבותות של אהבה וידידות כבר יותר מיובל שנים.

ידידי הנ"ל כבר חיבר כמה ספרים חשובים להראות נפלאות הבורא לקהל הצמאים לשמוע דברי אלקים חיים, ומאז ועד עתה יסד הסמינר 'בית חיה רחל' ושמו הולך לפניו בכשרונו המבורך להשקות מים חיים ביסודות אמרות ישראל, בבהירות הדעת ובצחות הלשון, בעניני אמונה ויראת שמים ואהבת ה', ועכשיו ליקט מדבריו עד שנעשה לספר שלם. ואף שאין ביכלתי לעיין בכתביו כפי הראוי באמת לכבודו, אבל מובטחני על חבר כמותו שאינו מוציא מתחת ידו דבר שאינו מתוקן, ומגלגלין זכות על ידי זכאי.

ועלי רק לברכו שכה יתן ה' וכה יוסיף להרבות להרבות כבוד שמים על ידי לימוד האמונה ויראת שמים, להגדיל תורה ולהאדירה.

בכבוד רב, ובידידות עוז,

מנחם חיים סלומון

RABBI E LIEBERMAN
37 GRASMERE STREET WEST
GATESHEAD NE8 1TS
ENGLAND
TEL: +44 191 477 1598
FAX: +44 191 440 2206

אלעזר ליברמן
בן אאמו"ר הגה"צ ר' יוסף נתן זצוק"ל
מו"ץ וראש הכשרות
בק"ק גייטסהעד יצ"ו

בס"ד

י"א אייר-יום כ"ו לעומר תשע"ח לפ"ק

It gives me great pleasure to write a few words to my dear revered friend, Rabbi Avrohom Katz שליט"א, the author of this unique book "וידעת היום".

We are living in challenging times of turmoil, where confusion is rampant - אור וחושך משתמשים בערבוביא - and the world at large is neither knowledgeable nor competent with many of our basic יסודות האמונה and השקפות .

נביא חבקוק , the בא חבקוק והעמידן על אחת" writes מכות כד: in גמרא . The taught us that everything depends on one principle "צדיק באמונתו יחיה" , a righteous person lives by his faith. Belief and faith are the basis of the entire תורה and מצות .

This book "וידעת היום " is based on Shiurim, which Rabbi Katz שליט"א has been giving in his seminary Beis Chaye Rochel for years, on a weekly basis . These Shiurim which contain true השקפות and יסודות הדת, are a weekly highlight due to their uniqueness in subject and delivery, where the most important and delicate topics are addressed in a unique enjoyable manner. Now that we have been fortunate enough to have these Shiurim published, we are deeply appreciative to Rabbi Katz for giving us the opportunity to read and benefit from them. I would thus recommend this book to be read by each and every individual.

May the author continue his עבודת הקודש with Berochoh and Hatzlochoh, and continue to enlighten the hearts and souls of so many, which will בס"ד bring the long awaited גאולה speedily in our times.

הכותב והחותם לכבוד התורה ולכבוד המחבר שליט"א,

אלעזר ליברמן

פסח אליהו פאלק	**Rabbi E. Falk**
מח"ס שו"ת מחזה אליהו	146 Whitehall Road
'זכור ושמור' על הלכות שבת	Gateshead, NE8 1TP
'עוז והדר לבושה' על צניעות דלבוש	England
מו"ץ בק"ק גייטסהעד יצ"ו	TEL: 0044-191-4782342

בס"ד

ה' אייר תשע"ח לפ"ק פה גייטסהעד יצ"ו.

הגיש לפני יד"נ מחנך דגול הרה"ג ר' אברהם טוביה הכהן כ"ץ שליט"א מיסד ומנהל סמינר "בית חיה רחל" דגייטסהעד ספר הנחוץ מאוד על יסודות האמונה וקראו בשם "וידעת היום". והוא שם המתאים לו מאוד מאחר שבו מברר מה קרה באמת ומה יש ללמוד מהעשר מכות, מקריאת י"ס, וממעמד הר סיני ועוד. מאורעות הללו הם הבסיס לכל עניני אמונה וע"י שיודע אדם אותם ידיעה ברורה הרי הוא מתקרב לדרך ה'. וזהו וידעת היום – ידיעה ברורה – והשבות אל לבבך.

ספר זה הוא פרי יגיעת שנים רבות של מחקר בחז"ל והעמקה בהחינוך המופלא שהונחל לנו ע"י כל אחד מתופעות גדולות הנ"ל. וכל דבריו מושרשים על יסודות איתנים שקבל מגדולי המשגיחים ושאר גדולי ישראל. ונתקיים בחיבור זה דברי הפסוק "כי שפתי כהן ישמרו דעת ותורה יבקשו מפיהו" באשר הוא בעצמו דוגמא חי של יהודי החי באמונה בצור העולמים.

הדור שלנו מלאה בלבולים ונסיונות קשות והנוער ורעב לדברים שישיב לו רגש האמונה, ולכן מוצאנו שספרים שיצאו לאחרונה בשפת המדינה בעניני אמונה נחטפו ונבלעו מיד כשיצאו לאור. ובכן תקוותי חזקה שכן יהא גורל ספר קדוש זה ורבים יתקרבו לאביהם שבשמים מכח האמת שיאיר עיניהם בדפי הספר. וידוע המחבר שליט"א שהוא בעל לשון בין בעל פה ובין בכתב ותענוג רוחני הוא לשמוע מוצא פיו וכן לקראות יצירי ידיו.

כן דברי יד"נ המאחל לו שפע של ברכה, ובכל אשר יפנה יצליח לרומם שם ה' בעולם.

הכותב וחותם לכבוד המוסרים נפשם עבור טהרת הקודש של דור הבא

פסח אליהו פאלק

פסח אליהו פאלק

Rabbi S.F. Zimmerman
Rov of Gateshead

שרגא פייבל הלוי זimmערמאן
אב"ד דק"ק גייטסהעד

ב"ד

ח' אייר תשע"ח

My dear friend and colleague Rabbi Avrohom Katz שליט"א of Gateshead, Principal of Beis Chaya Rochel Seminary and Manhig of Beis Ḥamedrash Ahavas Yisroel is about to publish a book entitled 'וידעת היום'. The book outlines the fundamental essentials of אמונה which each and every Jewish person must know.

The book is written in a very clear manner that elucidates this all important fundamental of Yahadus. It is apt that Rabbi Katz has written this book as he is living example of a בעל אמונה and embodies the principles of אמונה. I have read the book and highly recommend it as an essential classic.

May this book be a catalyst to strengthen our אמונה and may הקב"ה bentsch Rabbi Katz with much continued כח and סייעתא דשמיא to continue all his wonderful work and הרבצת התורה in good health.

החותם בכל ברכת התורה

95 Bewick Road, Gateshead, NE8 1RR
Tel: 0191 477 1847 Fax: 0191 477 7688

Table of Contents

Foreword 13

ONE: Introduction 17

TWO: Debilitating Doubt – Gone Forever 21

THREE: Levels of Knowledge 25

FOUR: More on Knowing 31

FIVE: Knowledge and *Emunah* 35

SIX: The Impossible Dream 40

SEVEN: The Great Escape 45

EIGHT: A Dawn like No Other 51

NINE: Ten Mighty Lessons 54

TEN: Expert Opposition 58

ELEVEN: Divine Intervention 62

TWELVE: A Closer Look at Divine Control 66

THIRTEEN: Divine Control in History 71

FOURTEEN: The Nature of the Unnatural 75

FIFTEEN: The Lock Is Sprung 81

SIXTEEN: The Key to Popularity 85

SEVENTEEN: Measure for Measure 91

EIGHTEEN: The Most Reluctant Leader 101

NINETEEN: The Truth 108

TWENTY: The Whole Truth 115
TWENTY-ONE: And Nothing but the Truth 120
TWENTY-TWO: No *Protektzia* 126
TWENTY-THREE: The Greatest Event in History 132
TWENTY-FOUR: Mitzvos That Testify 138
TWENTY-FIVE: More Mitzvos from Hashem 145
TWENTY-SIX: The Future Revealed 154
TWENTY-SEVEN: Prophecies That Defy the Odds 161
TWENTY-EIGHT: The Most Unlikely 168
TWENTY-NINE: The New Car 174
THIRTY: Seven Interdependent Systems 181
THIRTY-ONE: *Ales B'seder?* Is Everything Okay? 186
THIRTY-TWO: A Glimpse at Yourself 192
THIRTY-THREE: Observations of an Observant Jew 200
THIRTY-FOUR: The Accuracy of Our Transmission 209

Foreword

With endless gratitude to *Hashem Yisbarach*, I am delighted to offer the book *Now I Know* to the Jewish public.

The book has been twenty years in the making, and even longer in the thinking, and follows the three published books: *Designer World*, *Amazing World*, and *Wondrous World*. In truth, this book should have come first. Before the Exodus from Egypt and the Revelation at Sinai, knowledge of Hashem was gained primarily through observation of the created world; its design, complexity, and order. This followed the path of Avraham our father. Indeed, the path to knowledge of Hashem was *The Heavens declare the glory of G-d and the expanse of the sky tells of His Handiwork* (*Tehillim* 19:2).

Following the Exodus and the Revelation, our knowledge of Hashem is now rooted in the direct communication that we were privileged to receive, and the direct testimony witnessed by the entire Jewish Nation.

Ever since, we are enjoined to remember those events on a daily basis, and they form the twin pillars of empirical evidence that are our exclusive and unique heritage. Now that we possess that solid evidence – the only "religion" to so do, observation of the created world and details of the phenomena have taken their place in the command to love Hashem, as described by the Rambam, *The Almighty has commanded us to love and fear Him; as it says, "You should love Hashem your G-d" and "Hashem your G-d you should fear." What is the method by which one can come to love and fear Him? When one reflects on His deeds and His great and wonderful creation, and discerns and discovers the limitless wisdom contained therein – immediately he is gripped by admiration and love for the Creator...* (Hilchos Yesodei HaTorah 2:1-2). Our primary obligation now is to absorb the solid evidence gained from study of our Torah, the most accurate historical document in existence, which describes the events that give us our unique claim.

Hence, the material contained in this book is the more fundamental of the two themes; first comes knowledge of Hashem and then the love of Hashem. This book seeks to explore and explain the cast-iron evidence that enables us to know Hashem, it clarifies the huge gulf that separates us from all other religions, and galvanizes our ability to know Hashem.

Those who work in the field of Jewish education will know that all too often, *emunah* is assumed, spoken about, and demanded, without explaining the basis of that belief, or presenting the granite-base on which that belief rests. That is not Hashem's wish. Our Torah states unequivocally, *You have been shown, in order to know that Hashem, He is the G-d, there is none beside Him* (Devarim 4:35).

Very often, belief means wishful thinking and hoping but

without solid knowledge, and that belief often remains ethereal and insubstantial. This is not what Hashem wants! He has given us our national treasure – priceless solid knowledge – the prized possession of our People. *Israel* reads similarly to *is real*. This book presents the facts that allow us to know that reality.

As such, it is hoped that this book will find favor in the minds and hearts of all Klal Yisrael, from all circles; young and old, schools, yeshivos, seminaries, *kollelim*, and communities, for knowledge of Hashem is everyone's legacy.

The chapters of the book are based on lectures that have been given over the past twenty years to all manner of groups, both in Gateshead and further afield; and primarily as a fixture in the curriculum of the seminary, as well as to *bachurim*.

Enormous thanks have to be given to my *rebbi*, Rav Mattisyahu Salomon *shlit"a*, who has encouraged the writing of the book all the way through. It was with his guidance that the material was first given in lecture form, and it is our ardent wish that he should continue strengthening and inspiring Klal Yisrael in good health for many years *ad mei'ah v'esrim*.

The Gateshead community has been a wonderfully fertile and welcoming environment to bring up a family amongst inspired, idealistic, and generous people, all dedicated to living a full Torah life. The *kehillah* is blessed to enjoy the leadership of Rav Shraga Feivel Zimmerman *shlit"a* who, with his *ayin tovah*, encourages and rejoices in the flourishing growth of this unique *makom Torah*. His active encouragement throughout this project has been of immense value.

Particular thanks go to my dear friend R' Dovid Morgan, whose expertise in the publishing world and at Lehmann's World of Seforim has been invaluable.

As I struggle to survive in the computer age, I actually wrote this book in long hand with a Pilot 0.4mm black pen on lined paper – and the trusty and capable secretary who faithfully typed every word was Mrs. Chaya Royde, who deserves every thanks and *brachah*.

My dear wife and family, together with my revered colleagues in seminary, have been a constant source of support and encouragement, and no words of thanks could do justice to everything that I owe them. May Hakadosh Baruch Hu bless them with everything good, in best health and happiness *ad mei'ah v'esrim*.

The book has been dedicated to the memory of my dear older brother, *Habachur* Yitzchok Efraim *a"h*, who was the first in our family to make the spiritual journey from Leeds to Gateshead, with our parents' active encouragement, and in whose idealistic footsteps we humbly followed. Whatever we are is, in no small measure, thanks to his example, and it is right, therefore, that he should receive the eternal credit of bringing *Yidden* from all around the world closer to their Father in Heaven. *Yehi zichro baruch*.

ג' פ' אמור תשע"ח פה גייטסהעד יצ"ו

May 1, 2018

ONE
Introduction

Go to the mall. Look around at the swanky storefronts; listen to the self-assured pitches of suave salesmen, each one claiming that his line is the highest quality at the lowest prices. Watch the customer make his choice and then confidently swipe plastic. He hopes he has attained value for his money, but he is not overly concerned that he could have received a better deal elsewhere. What is at stake? A small amount of cash. For better or for worse, at least he has the product. If he is not happy with his purchase, he will be wiser next time. No harm done.

Go to the mall of religions. There you will find a dazzling array of competing products. Behind each of the hundreds of storefronts stands its representative dressed in his distinctive costume, seeking to attract the inquisitive passerby. With raucous cries, impassioned pleas, and eyes flashing sincerity, each salesman extols the virtues of his products. In the midst of the clamor, one word can be heard repeatedly. Everyone is using it. Truth.

"Come to the true religion," "We are truth." The potential purchaser is confused and bewildered. How can so many diametrically opposed views represent truth? By definition, truth is something that is in accordance with fact or reality. If many of the proffered religions are mutually exclusive ("if I am right, you are wrong; if you are correct, I am incorrect"), how can they all be true? And if all are claiming to be true, how do I know which – if any – are absolutely, truly true?

Now, if we were just casual observers in this interesting phenomenon of claims and counter-claims, we could – like passing tourists – observe the scene with a mixture of cynicism and humor. We could take our pick, make our purchase, and hope for the best. No harm done.

But we are Jews, and Jews make that strong unequivocal claim, "*Asher nassan lanu Toras emes.*" We call our Torah "The Law of Truth." On Simchas Torah, we jump up and down and declare with great passion, *Moshe emes v'soraso emes* – "Moshe is true and his Torah is true." As Jews, we are all in that mall. We have the greatest interest in knowing that our proclaimed "Truth" is absolute and unique.

Furthermore, to say "No harm done" is hardly a reflection of the facts. "No harm done" is if you are buying towels, or phones, or even a car. Even if it's not the plushest towel or the smoothest driving car, you'll still manage to dry your hands or get to where you want to go. But if one is in the market for a belief system and chooses wrongly? The harm is infinite! The life of a Jew is a commitment that spans his entire existence on Earth, and will affect every single aspect of that life. It will cost money and discipline his every movement and activity. The Torah places restrictions on every area of endeavor, and imposes demands that are inviolable. Ultimately, a Jew is expected to sacrifice his most treasured possession – his very own life – rather than transgress the central tenets of his belief. To commit oneself to a life of Judaism, one has to know with a cast-iron certainty that its claim of truth is indeed absolutely true.

Just to make it even more compelling, the Torah makes very specific promises of blessings and curses which are contingent on our observance of the Torah's laws. There is everything to gain – for eternity – from faithful adherence; and all to lose – again for eternity – by dereliction of our duties. You can be casual about purchasing a towel, easygoing when choosing a car – but there is no room for equivocation with something that will affect your life. You cannot be sanguine about your eternity! We have to know.

And therein lies the answer. In the single word "know" lies the key to the fundamental difference that distinguishes Judaism from every single religion, creed, or belief on the face of the earth.

To know means to be absolutely sure of something as a result of observing, asking, or being informed. There is all the difference in the world between knowing something as a result of direct and clear observation, and believing, which is a feeling that something exists or is true, without any proof. As will be explained, whereas every religion without exception is based and relies on "belief" or "faith," Judaism is unique in resting on a rock-solid foundation of knowledge – events observed by a whole nation.

If you're into politics, you know that the speeches of prominent politicians are carefully crafted, and subtle messages are sown into the text by the repeated use of a single phrase. The more the phrase is repeated, the stronger the message intended.

President Obama's famous repetition of the word "change" in his 2008 election campaign struck a chord with an electorate eager for change. The more frequently the word is used, the greater its prominence in the mind of the speaker, and subsequently, he hopes, in the ear of the listener.

In the Torah given to us by Hashem, the word "know," in reference to our perception and acceptance of G-d, is used more often than any other word. The word "know," as in absolute knowledge, is emphasized and re-emphasized as the one single fundamental on which our whole acceptance and allegiance to G-d is based.[1]

The function of this book is to clearly delineate the many aspects and examples of that knowledge, unique to Judaism, on which the truth of Judaism is constructed.

It is the sincere desire of the writer that after having read this book and absorbed the facts, the reader will feel secure in his acceptance of Hashem, be liberated from doubts, and with that newfound freedom, be able to live his Jewish life with security and happiness.

To borrow a phrase from Yisro, who, after hearing from his son-in-law Moshe the events of the Exodus firsthand, exclaimed, "Now I know that Hashem is the greatest of all gods!" (Shemos 18:11). That knowledge is the legacy of every Jew.

---

1.   *You have been shown in order to* know *that Hashem, He is the G-d, there is none beside Him* (Devarim 4:25).
You shall know *this day and take to your heart that Hashem – He is the G-d – in the Heavens above and on the Earth below, there is none other* (ibid. 4:39).

TWO
Debilitating Doubt – Gone Forever

To be in doubt is not a good place to be. Suppose you are in a store to buy a suit. Facing you are two similar suits; one is slightly more expensive, but the color that you like. The alternative is cheaper, but the color is not what you fancy. You cannot decide.

Or perhaps you have to choose a yeshivah. The large one is the place where your friends are going. Peer pressure is a powerful pull. On the other hand, there is a smaller yeshivah with an excellent reputation, in which the *talmidim* are able to develop a close association with the *rebbeim* – but none of your friends are keen on going there. Should you follow your friends, and sacrifice your genuine progress – or should you do what is in your best interest, and courageously create new friendships? You cannot decide.

Imagine that a *shidduch* has been suggested for you, and you have met the potential partner now several times, but you are not sure. Everything seems fine, sort of, but there are several little niggling points that cause you disquiet. On one hand, logic would seem to dictate yes; but on the other hand, you wake up in the morning – the moment of truth and clearest thinking – with a distinct reluctance to commit yourself. You cannot decide.

Anyone who has suffered from indecision will know only too well the debilitating impact it produces. Your mind is constantly preoccupied – should I, shouldn't I; the dilemma monopolizes your thoughts, paralyzes your mind, and stultifies your progress. If you were a car, your engine would be racing while your gears are not engaged. There is no shortage of sound, but neither is there forward motion.

What is worse, even when a decision *is* made, as inevitably it must be, the indecision remains. Did I make the correct decision? Recrimination and regret are the legacy of doubtful decisions. Whoever experiences doubt entertains one overriding desire: *I wish that someone, whose wisdom and experience I trust implicitly, could just* tell *me what to decide! Then I would know for sure, the debilitating doubt would disappear, and I could start living again.*

The larger the issue causing the doubt, the bigger the impact. Indecision on what breakfast cereal to choose will have minimal consequences. A dilemma in a *shidduch* decision will be seen as potentially affecting one's future life. Imagine, therefore, the ramifications of doubts affecting one's belief.

Picture someone who has grown up as a religious Jew, who has always faithfully followed religious practices, and who proudly identifies himself in every detail of external appearance and demeanor as a religious Jew. He will likely have received a solid Jewish education, and even more, be able to teach others who are less knowledgeable. However, through no fault of his own, no one ever bothered to explain to him the rock-solid truths on which Judaism rests. He may have been educated in a system in which knowledge of Hashem is assumed, in which acceptance of core beliefs are presumed, where a magic wand of *"emunah"* is waved over any disturbing question.

Consequently, at some point, an unexpected and troublesome thought may drop into his head. "How do I know it's true?" The thought might be devastating; he has never had these thoughts before. He does not know how to react. It is as if someone has pulled the rug from under his feet. He feels he cannot ask anyone, cannot share his sudden dilemma with anyone – for sure they will think him a *rasha*, so he tries to answer it himself.

And, unarmed with the essential information, not in possession of the vital knowledge, he may be thrown into doubt. Not doubt about a suit, a yeshivah, or a *shidduch*, but a doubt that concerns his very own existence; questions about the most basic fundamentals that underpin his every action as a religious Jew. Can there be anything more debilitating than that? The doubt will wake up with him and be his constant unwelcome companion until the day's end. It will plague him and haunt him and threaten to destroy his life.

If only his doubts could be resolved. If only he could be sure. Absolutely sure. Then he would be the happiest person in the world! Life would be great; there would be purpose in his stride, confidence in his life. He would perform mitzvos with conviction, with energy, and with joy.

Think about it. Does Hashem wish for us to be tormented by uncertainty, wallowing in a perennial state of doubt? Surely not! Logic demands that since Hashem is described as *compassionate and gracious, slow to anger and abundant in kindness and truth, preserver of kindness for thousands of generations...* (*Shemos* 34:6-7), He would want us to be energized with absolute clarity about His existence. We can safely posit that Hashem, about Whom it is said, *The Holy One, blessed is He, wished to confer merit upon Israel, therefore He gave them Torah and mitzvos in abundance* (*Mishnayos Makkos* 3:16), would wish us, His people, to be armed with all the information necessary to commit ourselves to His service – which requires dedicating our every action, our money, our very lives – with total rock-solid conviction. He would not want us to be plagued with even an atom of doubt or stymied by indecision. He would not want us to keep guessing.

The purpose of this book is to show clearly and convincingly that all the information that we require to be *yod'ei Shemecha* – "knowers of Your Name" is available to everyone, is clearly stated in the Torah, and is the treasured legacy of every Jew.

Armed with this knowledge, doubt and indecision (which will be explained, are the primary weapons of our implacable foe, Amalek) will be forever banished, consigned to breakfast cereals and suits, and we shall be able to live life fully and in joy.

Serve Hashem with gladness, come before Him with joyous song, know that Hashem, He is G-d... (*Tehillim* 100:2-3).

THREE
Levels of Knowledge

In the *brachah* that we recite after learning Torah, we state, *...Who gave us the Torah of truth...* Now, many religions claim that theirs is the true religion. How do we know that Judaism is the "real" true religion?

As mentioned before, there is a world of difference between knowledge and that which people call faith. Faith is a strong belief in a religion, based on spiritual feeling rather than proof. Knowledge means to be aware of a fact through observation, inquiry, or information.

All religions in the world are based on faith, believing something to be true, or wishing something to be true, but with no way of proving their belief to be true. Judaism, in complete contrast, is based on rock-solid knowledge.

Consider the following four levels of knowing anything. We shall begin with level two (level one will be explained shortly). Imagine that two people are walking toward a room, arguing fiercely. The room is entirely empty, with no other entrance. They enter the room and shut the door. Suddenly, a gunshot is heard from the room. The door opens and one man walks out, a smoking gun in his hand, saying, "Ha! He deserved that!" Running into the room, you see the other man lying – not very much alive – on the floor. The man holding the gun is arrested, and admits to the crime. He explains his motive. The gun is his. The shot that dispatched the victim was fired at an angle that precludes the victim having shot himself, and the perpetrator of the wicked crime has long been threatening to rid himself of his enemy once and for all. Later, at his trial, the twelve-person jury has no hesitation in finding the accused guilty. And indeed, why should they hesitate? There is no regular court in the world that would not find him guilty. All the evidence points accusingly in his direction, although no one saw him commit the crime. That level of knowing is called circumstantial evidence.

Then you have level three, a lesser form of knowledge, called hypothesis. This is a supposition of proposed explanation made on the basis of limited evidence, as a starting point for further investigation. For example, someone finds a tooth in his back garden while digging for potatoes. Excitedly, he calls in the archaeologists, who examine the fossil with magnifying glasses. On the basis of their preliminary examination, they surmise that the tooth is indeed ancient. On the basis of this historic find, the archaeologists claim the discovery of the remains of a prehistoric brontaclotapix, at least 300 million years old. That claim is a hypothesis.

The learned hypothesis evaporates when the youngest member of the family sheepishly admits that having placed his loose tooth under his pillow, and failing to find money the next morning, he thought he might have better luck by burying his tooth in the garden, where the tooth-fairies live.

The lowest rung, level four, are the tooth-fairies themselves, together with all other myths. A myth is a widely held but false belief completely lacking any evidence. All ancient Greek and Roman mythology – St. George killing a dragon; and a portly figure wearing a red *bekeshe* and a red hat with a white pom-pom easing himself down the chimney, a sack of toys nonchalantly slung over his shoulder – fit comfortably into this make-believe category.

At the very top stands level one, all alone. This is the level of empirical evidence – evidence based on verifiable observation and experience. It is the evidence demanded by the Torah. On our second level, where the two men were walking into the empty room, everyone would declare the gun-owner guilty. Everyone except the Torah. No witnesses saw the crime. No one warned the culprit. Circumstantial evidence is not accepted in Torah law.

By the testimony of two witnesses…shall the condemned man be put to death (*Devarim* 16:6).

Hashem, so to speak, keeps the laws of the Torah. He wished to communicate to His chosen people, and allow them to see and hear His Presence so that they can attain "level one knowledge" of His existence. *I shall take you to Me as a people, and I shall be a G-d to you; and you shall* know *that I am Hashem your G-d…* (*Shemos* 6:7). How will they *know*?

By seeing and hearing Him, as He promised in advance that they would. *Hashem said to Moshe, "Behold! I come to you in the thickness of the cloud, so that the people will hear as I speak to you"* (ibid. 19:9).

Hashem said to Moshe... "Let them be prepared for the third day, for on the third day Hashem shall descend in the sight of the entire people on Mount Sinai" (ibid. 19:10-11).

It happened exactly as promised. *"...you have seen that I have spoken to you from Heaven"* (ibid. 20:19). There were not just two witnesses, but 600,000, who, together with their families, saw and heard Hashem speak directly to them, announcing His existence. The whole entirety of the Jewish Nation saw this Revelation with their own eyes, heard the sounds (and even saw the sounds; *The entire people saw the sounds...* [ibid. 20:15]) with their own ears, and everyone shared the identical experience. That is empirical evidence and that is knowledge. It is to that unique experience that the Torah refers when it says, *You have been shown, in order to know that Hashem, He is G-d, there is no one beside Him* (*Devarim* 4:35).

The Torah uses the word "know" repeatedly and pointedly. When Avraham Avinu asked Hashem for an assurance that he and his children would inherit the Land of Israel, Hashem responded with the expression, *yadoa teida – Know with certainty that your offspring shall be aliens in a land not their own, and they will serve them and they will oppress them – four hundred years. Also, the nation that they will serve, I shall judge, and afterward they will leave with great wealth* (*Bereishis* 15:13-15). The passage referring to the Exodus is prefaced with the words, *you will know with certainty.*

It is therefore no wonder that the events surrounding the Exodus, and particularly the plagues themselves, are prefaced

Levels of Knowledge

with and inexorably connected to the word "know," which is used repeatedly throughout the *pesukim*.[1]

Our belief in Hashem is firmly anchored in a solid foundation of knowledge. We have been shown in order to know. That is the very highest level of knowledge, and the privilege is uniquely ours.

We know the place, the year, the month, and the day of the week that this Revelation took place. It was approximately one hundred generations ago – that is one hundred photographs around your living room (a mere yesterday compared to the mythical 300-plus million years), and we are the direct descendants of the people who experienced this empirical knowledge and evidence.

No other nation in the world – at any time, in any place – has experienced a similar or comparable revelation, or even claims to have done so. The event is simply too massive to claim that it happened if it did not. You cannot superimpose an event of such magnitude on the tapestry of world history if it did not happen.

We, the Jewish People, have been granted a unique privilege: knowledge, based on empirical evidence, of Hashem. What about

---

1. *I shall take you to Me for a people, and I shall be a G-d to you, and you shall know that I am Hashem your G-d...* (Shemos 6:7).

Before the plague of blood, Hashem announced, *So says Hashem – through this shall you know that I am Hashem* (ibid. 7:17).

Before the plague of wild animals, Hashem announced, *And on that day I shall set apart the land of Goshen upon which My people stands, that there shall be no swarm there, so that you will know that I am Hashem in the midst of the land* (ibid. 8:18).

Finally, before the plague of hail, Hashem announced, *For this time I shall send all My plagues against your heart, and upon your servants, and your people, so that you shall know that there is none like Me in all the world* (ibid. 9:14).

other religions? At which level would we place their beliefs? The answer, unhappily for them, is at level four, a widely held but false belief, completely lacking any evidence.

"Mr. Christian, you claim that your leader was the son of G-d. Prove it."

"You have to have faith!"

"Mr. Moslem, you claim that your founder was the true prophet. Prove it."

"You just have to believe!"

The claims of all religions are based on the say-so of one charismatic individual or his enthusiastic followers who gathered a group of gullible admirers around them, convincing them of their veracity. Proof, please? None. Just pure faith based on wishful thinking. A vaporous cloud built on a puff of smoke.

Three times a day, we declare in the *Aleinu* prayer, *He has not made us like the nations of the lands, and has not placed us like the families of the Earth…for they bow to vanity and emptiness… True is our G-d and there is nothing beside Him, as it is written in the Torah, "You are to know this and take to your heart that Hashem is the only G-d, in heaven above and on earth below, there is none other."*

Our knowledge is our precious and unique legacy, the priceless facts that every Jew must know.

FOUR
More on Knowing

We all claim to know things. When we say we know something – not in some deep philosophical sense, but on a practical everyday level – how *do* we know it? On any given day, you might tell someone that you know your living room is painted yellow, that you know that the earth goes around the sun, that you know the way to London. Clearly, these different assertions are based on different ways of knowing. What are they?

The first method of knowing something is, of course, through personal experience. You know that your living room is painted yellow because you have been in that room and saw it was yellow. Similarly, you know what a bird is, how gravity works, and how to travel to the nearest town all by direct experience. You meet someone you have never seen before, you ask him his name, and the next time you see the person, you recognize and identify him by name and the response is positive; you can say you know the person.

The second way to know something is by authority. That is, you rely on some source of information, believing it to be reliable, when you have no experience of your own. Therefore, almost every person who attended school believes that the earth goes around the sun, even though very few people would be able to tell you how anyone could even detect that motion. You are relying on authority if, when asked if you know the way to London, you answer yes and pull out a map. You might be able to personally test the map's reliability by using it to navigate to London, but until you do, you are relying on authority. Similarly, if someone asks if you know a telephone number, you would pull out the phone book and say, "Here it is – I know the number," though you have no personal experience, never having dialed that number and spoken to the bearer of the name. But you have used the phone book on many occasions, and using the numbers listed, successfully connected to the correct person. You rely on the phone book implicitly. It possesses impeccable authority.

Yet, it is still incomparable to knowledge by experience. The Exodus from Egypt, together with the Revelation at Mount Sinai, were the greatest experiences of "knowing Hashem" in history and are unique to the Jewish People, forming the bedrock on which our faith is built. They saw. They heard. They felt. And just as someone who stood at the foot of the majestic Alps in Switzerland would never forget the experience, so too, the Jews will never forget the Exodus and Mount Sinai, experiences that are many times more profound.

It was stated earlier that circumstantial evidence is inadmissible in Jewish law. A witness is a person who sees an event taking place. Seeing is knowing. Not surprisingly, the Hebrew word for "knowing" is ד׳ע. The word for a witness is comprised of those same letters, reversed: ע׳ד. You can only be accepted as an

More on Knowing

עד if you דע. Amazingly, but again, not surprisingly, the sentence that encapsulates Jewish acceptance of Hashem as our G-d, *Hear O Israel, Hashem is our G-d, Hashem is One* (*Devarim* 6:4), is written in the Torah with an enlarged *ayin* in the word *shema* and an enlarged *daled* in the word *echad*. Together, those letters formulate the words עד – *witness* and דע – *know*. Our knowledge of Hashem is built on our collective witness and knowledge.

It is precisely because of this that Hashem can demand our loyalty and service as His special nation. No less is stated specifically, when after describing the pivotal events of the Exodus and Mount Sinai, Moshe Rabbeinu tells the Jewish People, *"You shall know this day; take to your heart that Hashem, He is the G-d, in heaven above and on the earth below – there is none other. You shall observe His decrees and His commandments that I command you this day..."* (*Devarim* 4:39-40).

It also explains why, after experiencing the presence of Hashem with such unequivocal clarity, we can expect very specific and not always pleasant consequences for disloyalty and failure to adhere to our obligations. No one could gaze at the Swiss Alps and fail to have that picture indelibly imprinted on his memory. No one could gain the level of knowledge granted to our own people, and claim not to know.

Bearing all this in mind, it is worthwhile to hear a story that focuses very clearly on the tragedy of people, who, perhaps through no fault of their own, do not know. I was once traveling by plane back from Eretz Yisrael to England. Seated next to me was a man who identified himself as Jewish but did not look religious. In the course of our conversation, he told me he lives in Baltimore, and had been to Israel to visit his son, who was studying in a yeshivah. Noting his bare head, I asked him how he feels about his son's love for the Jewish religion. "Oh, that's fine," he said. "Religion is a matter of feeling, and he's got a strong feeling for it. I don't." When I suggested that the Jewish religion is definitely more than feeling, and actually based on definite knowledge and very specific obligations with concrete consequences, he would have none of it. "Not at all – it's a matter of feeling. It all depends on your feelings; he has the feelings, and I don't."

How can we evaluate the tragedy of our own brethren, who, starved of knowledge, erroneously think that acceptance of Hashem and His Torah is an optional exercise, like whether to vote in an election?! We cannot change the past. But we can present the evidence, demonstrate the knowledge, and build the future, a future in which *...the earth will be filled with knowledge of Hashem as water covering the sea-bed* (*Yeshayahu* 11:9).

FIVE
Knowledge and Emunah

A very crucial question needs to be clarified. If the belief of a Jew is knowledge-based, with empirical evidence forming the bedrock of our knowledge of Hashem, then what exactly is *emunah*? Rabbi Yigal Shekalim, in his groundbreaking book, *Hashem L'negdi*, asks this question, and states that he received an answer from Rav Don Segal, who in turn heard it from Rav Shach *zt"l*, who equally posed the question to the Brisker Rav *zt"l*, who admitted that he had pondered over the question, and had asked his own father, Rav Chaim of Brisk *zt"l* – who had answered that *emunah* begins where knowledge ends. True, our acceptance of Hashem is built primarily on the solid knowledge gained at the Exodus from Egypt and the Revelation at Mount Sinai; and indeed, that was the purpose of those profound events. However, there are many things that are beyond the limits of knowledge, things that cannot be seen, heard, or fully comprehended by our limited intellect. And it is our acceptance of the truths of those facts and concepts that are included in *emunah*.

To understand the nature of Hashem is beyond the limits of our mind. Indeed, our Talmudic sources forbid a person to ponder on the essence of Hashem, or to try and elucidate what there was prior to the creation of this world (*Chagigah* 9b). To have *emunah* is to accept that our intellect is limited, but nevertheless everything the Torah tells us is true. For example, every Jewish person accepts the Ramban's Thirteen Principles of Faith. They are printed in our siddur at the end of Shacharis, and many recite them on a daily basis. Those Thirteen Principles encapsulate the nature of belief in G-d, the authenticity of the Torah, its validity and immutability, and man's responsibility and ultimate reward. Not everything in the list of thirteen is "known." "We believe in complete faith in the coming of Messiah" – although we have not seen him, and do not know his identity. "We believe with perfect faith that there will be a resuscitation of the dead whenever the wish emanates from the Creator" – although this is something we have not yet witnessed. This is *emunah* – absolute acceptance of prophecies and predictions – facts beyond the scope of human experience.

The relationship between *yediah* – "knowledge," and *emunah* – "faith," is best expressed by the Prophet Hoshe'a, in a statement that is recited daily while wrapping the strap of *tefillin* around our fingers: *I will betroth you to Me forever; I will betroth you to Me with righteousness, with justice and kindness and mercy; and I will betroth you to me in fidelity* (emunah) *and you will know Hashem* (*Hoshe'a* 2:21-22). The twin concepts of *yediah* and *emunah* literally go hand in hand. We have a responsibility, repeated again and again in the Torah, to *know* Hashem. Our acceptance of that knowledge together with our acceptance of everything we are taught in the Torah, whether we understand it or otherwise, whether it is within our ability to grasp or further than the boundaries of our intellect – that loyal acceptance and willingness to live and even die for its demands – that is called *emunah*.

The word *emunah* also means loyal, or trustworthy – worthy of our trust. After reciting the *haftorah* each Shabbos, we say, *Trustworthy are You, Hashem our G-d, and trustworthy are Your words. Not one of Your words is turned back to its origin unfulfilled, for You are G-d, trustworthy and compassionate King. Blessed are You, Hashem, the G-d Who is trustworthy in all His words.*

Rav Samson Raphael Hirsch *zt"l*, in his commentary on Chumash, explains the phrase, *V'he'emin baHashem* (*Bereishis* 15:6), to mean that Avraham placed his whole confidence in G-d. In the course of his explanation, he states: "*Emunah* is not belief. [The word belief] robs this central idea of Jewish consciousness of its real conception. Belief is an act of mind, is often only an opinion, is always believing something to be true by reason or judgment, and the assurance of somebody else. In making religion into a belief, and then making that cardinal point of religion believing in the truth of a certain thesis quite untenable to the intelligence, religion has been banned from everyday life…and made into a catechism of words of belief which will be demanded as a passport for entry into the next world… In contrast, *v'he'emin baHashem* is…leaving yourself entirely to Him, giving yourself up as a plastic material to be molded by G-d; in short, to refer yourself and all you have entirely to G-d. To respond to a spoken statement with "amen" does not mean to declare it to be true, but rather to give yourself up to the truth expressed in the sentence, to make it your own, and to vow to allow yourself to be guided by it."

Our greatest leader, Moshe Rabbeinu, is described by Hashem, *In My entire house he is the trusted one* (*Bamidbar* 12:7). The complete trust that Hashem had in Moshe was reflected in the trust that the Jewish People had for their great leader. In fact, that particular verse is translated in *Targum Yonasan ben Uziel* as "*In My House of Israel, he is the trusted one.*" The Jewish People knew Moshe. They saw him, heard him, learned from him, interacted with him, knew his family, and they trusted him; they knew him to be totally reliable and trustworthy. That absolute confidence and trust lies in the word *emunah*.

When the Jewish People were battling with Amalek shortly after crossing the Red Sea, the Torah describes that Moshe stood visible to the fighters, with his hands raised high. His hands grew heavy, so they took a stone, put it under him, and he sat on it. Aharon and Chur supported his hands, one on each side. The Torah describes how Moshe remained with his hands "*emunah*" until sunset (*Shemos* 17:11-12). Here, the word *emunah* means "in faithful prayer." Trustworthy, loyal, reliable, dependable – all those admirable qualities form the essence of the word "*emunah.*"

Whenever a young couple marries, we wish them the merit to build a *bayis ne'eman b'Yisrael*, a faithful house in Israel. If we understand that the greatest quality that can exist between husband and wife is faithfulness, a complete trust that each has in the other's fidelity and loyalty which is unimpeachable and beyond question, then we understand our blessing to the newly married pair. That their home should incorporate that same fidelity that they have toward each other, to the standards and ideals of the Torah which they hope to incorporate into their new home.

The Jewish People are really the most fortunate of people. Their *emunah* is not wishful thinking, a cloud built on a cloud, an ephemeral idea built on intangible concepts, hoping, wishing something to be true, all without facts and foundation. Rather, it is the total confidence, the assuredness, the absolute certainty that everything stated in the Torah is true, and that in turn is firmly grounded in the empirical evidence of our own people, who saw with their eyes and heard with their ears the interaction of Hashem with themselves in the Exodus from Egypt and at the Revelation at Sinai.

SIX
The Impossible Dream

A very good friend of mine traveled by plane from Gateshead, in the Northeast of England, to Sao Paulo, in Brazil. During the long flight, in a novel attempt to occupy his mind productively, he tried to imagine how long this same journey would have taken in 1813, some two hundred years earlier. His findings were very interesting.

At the present time, England is serviced by a wonderful network of high-quality roads. The motorway system, with its wide, multi-lane smooth road surfaces, spans the length and breadth of the country. Service stations provide fuel, respite, and nourishment at regular intervals. In 1813, twelve years before the introduction of the first public steam-locomotive, the roads for the most part were dirt-tracks. Passengers would travel in horse-drawn coaches at an average speed of 10 mph. The coaches were unheated, uncomfortable, and always ran the risk of being held up by notorious highwaymen who robbed and pillaged, and would not hesitate to remove the wheels of the coach to facilitate their own getaway. Our passenger, safely arrived in Plymouth or perhaps Bristol after a two- or three-day journey from Gateshead, would now be ready to cross the Atlantic on the next available ship. Given that the first scheduled steam-powered ship was only introduced in 1838 ("The Savannah," the Americans claimed, was the first ship to cross the Atlantic in 1819, powered by steam), perforce, our intrepid traveler would have to undertake the perilous voyage in a sailing-ship. The famous Mayflower, when it sailed for the "New World" in 1620, took sixty-six days to cross the Atlantic. Even in the early 1800s, conditions were Spartan. The ship would be rolling and pitching, at the mercy of winds and storms, fragile and vulnerable in the heaving seas.

Weeks after embarking, our seasick passenger would gratefully put his feet on dry land on the East Coast of America, and contemplate the next epic leg of his journey. He had a choice of traveling overland down the thousands of miles to South America, or by yet another lengthy sea voyage. His total journey would have taken some three months. During that time, there would be no communication with home; his life would be in constant danger; he would have to purchase food on the way, or take ample provisions. (How many sandwiches for sixty-six days?) Finally, with immense relief and gratitude, our friend would arrive in Sao Paulo.

Imagine that you are there to greet him. Taking him aside, you tell him that you are a visitor from two centuries hence, and you would like to enlighten him about future travel. "I want you to know, that in two hundred years' time, you will be able to *daven* Shacharis in Gateshead, and Minchah on the same day in Sao Paulo. On the same day! Not only that, but in the metallic tube that will transport you through the air six miles high in the sky at 550 mph, you will be served a hot kosher meal with the very best *hechsher.*" You then remove your cell phone from your pocket. "With this little piece of metal, plastic (what is plastic?), and rubber, you will be able to communicate with your family back in England, and inform them that *baruch Hashem* you had an excellent flight, that you managed to sleep for a couple of hours, and that the immigration line is moving quite fast."

Your 1813 friend will look at you agape, entirely incapable of understanding what you are saying. He will not possess the frame of reference to comprehend the concepts. Fly? At 550 mph? Speak into metal? All in one day? Kosher food in the air? He will shake his head in bewilderment and incomprehension.

This scenario, lengthy though it may be, will help us understand the situation of our ancestors, the Bnei Yisrael in Egypt at the time of the servitude. The period of the Jewish enslavement lasted for a period of approximately one century.[1]

At the beginning of the enslavement, there will have been many who remembered their good times, their freedom and autonomy. With the passage of time, however, these memories will have faded, and as the older generation passes away, those memories will have completely disappeared. The later generations

---

1. The actual bondage of the Israelites did not begin before Levi, the last of Yosef's brothers, died in the year 2332, twenty years after the passing of Yosef. Hence, the actual servitude of the Jews lasted less than 116 years. While it is not known precisely when the slavery began, we know that it began before the birth of Miriam, sister of Moshe, since she was named after the *mirur*, or the bitterness of the Egyptian oppression. Miriam, who was four years older than Moshe, was born in 2361. Thus, the enslavement and oppression of the Jewish People lasted a minimum of eighty-seven years, but less than 116 years. (From *Legacy of Sinai*, by Rabbi Zechariah Fendel, published by the Rabbi Jacob Joseph School Press in 1981.)

were born into slavery. We can imagine that their life was one constant struggle for survival. We read in the harrowing accounts of our own families who endured the horrors of Nazi oppression, how difficult it was to maintain optimism and hope. Life in the purgatory of the camps was a bitter fight to remain alive – another day – *just one* day. Imagine that level of servitude and bondage for a *century*. Children born into slavery would have heard the traditions of their fathers concerning their noble origins, their original status, and their eventual redemption. However, in the midst of the whipping and relentless forced labor, their vision and ambitions would have been severely curtailed. When waking in the morning after an exhausted fitful sleep, what would be their thoughts and hope for the day? Perhaps the Egyptian taskmasters would be kind today and give them a plentiful supply of straw with which to make bricks. Maybe the officer assigned to their work battalion would not be one of the cruel ones, but would whip them a little less – and not on the sore, scarred skin. Perhaps there would be time to eat, to rest just a bit, before the next day's relentless, endless toil.

Imagine you would have gone to one of the slaves, someone born during that century of slavery, pulled him aside, and said, "I want to tell you some of the wonderful things that will happen to you and all your family in just a few years. Those terrible Egyptians will be punished by Hashem in an incredible series of plagues and punishments, the country will be devastated, and eventually your prison guards who beat and torture you will beg you to leave Egypt. Not only that, but when you leave, the Egyptians will give you all their money, their silver and gold. You will walk out of Egypt free men, and rich!" Your poor, downtrodden Jewish slave would look at you with a blank and disbelieving expression, completely unable to comprehend your words. "I don't understand – free? Rich? Out of Egypt? Plagues?" He would shake his head sadly and uncomprehendingly, and trudge back to his work, his bowed and sun-burned back submitting to the ever-present whip. He could not conceive of walking free out of his prison any more than our traveler could comprehend a Shacharis in Gateshead and a Minchah – on the same day – in Sao Paulo.

And it was in this situation of virtual and seeming helplessness that Hashem sent His promise to release the Jewish People. Hashem, Hashem alone, would spring the lock, and the wicked Egyptians would themselves urge their erstwhile slaves to freedom. It would be an unprecedented display of *yedias Hashem*.

SEVEN
The Great Escape

It can be the worst of times and the best of times. There is a custom that if a baby boy is born on Tishah B'Av, he receives the name Menachem (*Tashbatz* 3:8). The reason for this is that our sages tell us that Mashiach will be born on that day (*Talmud Yerushalmi, Brachos* 2:4). Hashem underpins quintessential Jewish optimism by choosing the day of the year suffused with tragedies of persecution and destruction as the birthday of the Redeemer of our people. In a similar fashion, while the Jews in Egypt were suffering from the seeming interminable slavery, Hashem was planning their salvation.

Among the many nations that occupy their homeland, there are numerous ways by which they gained their autonomy. Some developed peacefully, others occupied territory through military process, and still others simply overthrew the indigenous occupants, like a cuckoo settling into a nest and throwing out the resident eggs. The emergence of the Jewish People as an independent nation could not be so mundane. The nation that Hashem chose to be His flag-bearers had to emerge onto the world scene in a manner that would forever establish their unique role. In much the same way that a brilliantly beautiful butterfly, resplendent in its colors and shimmering translucence, emerges from its drab chrysalis and metamorphoses from its caterpillar form in a manner that no one could have predicted, so the Jewish People had to transform from a collection of servile slaves to proud and independent nationhood in a manner that no one could have predicted or effected. The Exodus from Egypt would be the unique metamorphosis – never replicated and never repeated – that would stamp this people with the indelible sign that would forever proclaim, *I am Hashem your G-d, Who has removed you from the land of Egypt to be a G-d unto you, I am Hashem your G-d* (*Bamidbar* 15:41).

The ten plagues that preceded the great Exodus would establish the solid knowledge of the existence of Hashem, which was the purpose of the great event. And who would be the leader and spokesman of the Jewish People at that pivotal time? It had to be a man of great qualities, yet so humble, he wouldn't want to lead; it had to be Moshe Rabbeinu. It is his reluctance to lead, as well as the sequence of events that followed, that help assure us that Hashem alone was the one and only responsible for our release.

The Torah tells us that the Jewish slaves in Egypt groaned under their incessant labor, and they cried out to Hashem. Their supplications did not go unheeded, and Hashem chose Moshe to be the leader. Together with his brother Aharon, they gathered the elders of the Jewish People, and repeated the words that Hashem had spoken to Moshe. They presented their credentials of reliability, and the elders were convinced of their authenticity. *And the people believed, and they heard that Hashem had remembered the Children of Israel and that He saw their affliction…* (*Shemos* 4:31).

We can imagine the anticipation that spread through the ranks of slaves. Like a cooling breeze on a sultry day, like an emerging sunbeam rippling through a golden cornfield, the news spread. "The Redeemer has arrived! Yes – it's true! He is going to speak to the mighty Pharaoh and demand our release! Our slavery is going to stop! We won't have to work!" The hope that had lain dormant for close to a century suddenly emerged, and like molten lava bubbling in an irresistible surge from the lip of a volcano, the thrill and excitement of expectation spread through the people.

Nothing could have prepared the Jews for the bitter disappointment that was to follow. Moshe and Aharon had courageously confronted Pharaoh and, in the name of Hashem, demanded that he release the Jews. Pharaoh professed not to know this G-d. In a statement of absolute denial, he stated defiantly, *"Who is Hashem that I should heed His voice to send out Israel? I do not know Hashem, nor will I send out Israel"* (ibid. 5:12). Then, adding insult to injury, he curtly chastised the two brothers for interfering with the Egyptian economy by causing the Jewish laborers to use fantasies of G-dly service as an excuse for laziness. Then came the hammer blow.

If the Jews could be thinking of freedom, then work conditions must be too relaxed. With unprecedented cruelty, Pharaoh converted intolerable demands into impossible ones. Until now, the Jewish slaves had been supplied with the mud and straw – raw materials – with which to fashion bricks. Now they would have to procure their own raw materials – an impossible task – and produce the same quota of bricks as hitherto. Imagine that you work in a car factory. From the various components that are transported by conveyor belt, you, together with your fellow workers, can assemble your car. How would you feel if a draconian edict was enacted that decreed that no longer would the conveyor belt deliver the components? You would have to construct those yourself. But the quota of completed cars must remain constant. Rummaging through scrap yards in a desperate search for rubber, plastic, glass, metal, wire, and fabric, the panic exacerbated by the relentless passage of time and cruel whips on your back, it would not take long for you to throw up your hands in resigned surrender.

This was the situation of the Jewish slaves. Their nascent dream of freedom had evaporated. Their slowly emerging hopes had crashed to the ground. The warm expectation of relaxation from their labor had been transformed into impossible harshness. And who did they blame? The very man in whom they had placed their hopes and whose mission had so badly failed. In their bitterness and pain, they accused Moshe and Aharon of aggravating their situation: *"You have made our very scent abhorrent in the eyes of Pharaoh and the eyes of his servants, to place a sword in their hands to murder us"* (ibid. 5:21).

Rav Samson Raphael Hirsch *zt"l* describes Moshe's feelings at that moment of despair. "Let us visualize the actual position at which Moshe now stood. His mission had completely misfired. Pharaoh had only become harsher and added derision to oppression. The people looked at Moshe and Aharon as deceivers, or at best, themselves deceived. Moshe himself had lost all confidence in himself – he would not be Moshe if his mistrust of his own ability was not deepened, if he did not think that he himself was to blame, that he had bungled his mission by handling it in the wrong way. What man would not have doubts of himself when he sees 600,000 innocent men cruelly tortured and cast down in utter despair through him!"

The question is why, in the Divine orchestration of events, did the situation have to become aggravated before improving? Why did Moshe's mission first have to result in abject failure before the Exodus could commence? In the response given by Hashem to Moshe's own heartfelt questioning, lies the foundation of the purpose of the Great Exodus. *Now you will see what I shall do to Pharaoh, for with a strong hand he will let them go, and through a strong hand he will drive them out of the land* (ibid. 6:1).

Rav Hirsch explains the answer. "This is just the moment for which I was waiting. This complete lack of power, this despair, must first be made evident; it must be first made clear that by ordinary human means, nothing, absolutely nothing, can be accomplished with Pharaoh. In the presence of the representatives of the people, Moshe and Aharon must stand there, completely stumped, and their inability to do anything clearly demonstrated, before the deliverance can commence as the sole work of G-d. Now that the very last trace of any natural means of help has disappeared, it is now apparent that Moshe is only the instrument of G-d, and the deliverance is stamped as the work of G-d, and G-d only."

It had to be made abundantly clear that no one – not even the much vaunted and long-awaited Redeemer – had the ability by himself to improve the situation. To the contrary, he only succeeded in aggravating the situation, making it so much worse. Now that it is clear to everyone that no human can do anything, that the Jews' situation was helpless and hopeless, now Hashem can intervene with a mighty hand and show that Hashem alone, and no one else, brought the Jewish People out of Egypt. There had to be a worst of times – in which human agencies were shown to be powerless – to contrast the best of times, in which everyone would know that Hashem alone released His nation from their bondage.

I will pass through the Land of Egypt, I and no angel; I will slay every firstborn in the land of Egypt, I and no Seraph; and I will execute judgment against all the gods of Egypt, I and no messenger; I, Hashem – it is I and no other (*Haggadah shel Pesach*).

EIGHT
A Dawn like No Other

After the deepest darkness came the dawn; Hashem opened a new chapter of events that would release the Jews with an unprecedented display of Divine intervention. *Has a g-d ever done miracles, bringing one nation out of another nation, with such tremendous miracles, signs, wonders, war, and a mighty hand and outstretched arm, and terrifying phenomena, as G-d did for you in Egypt, before your very eyes?* (*Devarim* 4:34). The ten plagues, described so graphically by the Torah, were the fulfillment of Hashem's promise to Moshe: *Now you shall see what I shall do to Pharaoh, for through a strong hand will he send them out, and with a strong hand will he drive them from his land* (*Shemos* 6:1).

The dazzling display of Divine might, carried out in full view of both the Jewish and Egyptian inhabitants of Egypt (*...before your very eyes*) had a purpose whose consequence extends until today – and for all time. *You shall know that I am Hashem your G-d* (ibid. 6:7). Not a day goes by without Jewish people mentioning the Exodus from Egypt. Seven days a year are spent actually reliving the events of the Exodus; passages from the Torah describing the Exodus are inscribed on parchment and inserted in the *tefillin* worn by Jewish men each morning; and the twice-daily recitation of the Shema includes mention of the Exodus, and its function as providing empirical evidence of Hashem's involvement in the affairs of man, and in particular, the Jewish Nation.

The Malbim,[1] in his commentary at the beginning of *Parshas Va'eira*, explains how during *Yetzias Mitzrayim*, Hashem interacted with worldly events in a dramatically different way than usual. Contrasting the different names by which Hashem identifies Himself, Hashem explained that until now, the great forefathers, Avraham, Yitzchak, and Yaakov, had experienced revelation of Hashem through limited, seemingly natural means. Now, with the four-letter proper name of Hashem, Moshe and the Jewish People would be privileged to gain a revelation of Hashem transcending the boundaries of nature. This miraculous dimension of Divine intervention would span the Exodus with its attendant ten plagues, the Revelation of Hashem at Mount Sinai, the forty-year odyssey through the desert, and the eventual successful conquering and settlement of the Land of Israel.

The evidence and experiences of that fifty-year period, all of which would involve every single member of the Jewish People – men, women, children, young and old – numbering into the millions, would form the bedrock of *yediah* on which our faith would be firmly attached. The level of revelation, the personal witness of so many people, would be an absolutely unique experience, unprecedented in all of human history and

---

1. Abbreviation of Meir Leib ben Yechiel Michel (Weiser), 1809-1879, author of *HaTorah V'hamitzvah*. He was considered one of the great intellects of his time, and served as Chief Rabbi of Romania.

unparalleled in any man-made religion or culture, and would serve as an eternal reference to the fact that *I shall take you to Me for a people, and I shall be a G-d to you; and you shall know that I am Hashem your G-d* (*Shemos* 6:6).

NINE
Ten Mighty Lessons

All numbers have special meaning according to Jewish teaching, but the number ten is extra special. The Maharal,[1] in his commentary on *Pirkei Avos* 5:1, explains that the number ten indicates the presence of Hashem. Whether with the utterance of creation, the ten tests of Avraham, the ten men required for a *minyan*, the Ten Commandments, or the holiest day of the year – Yom Kippur – falling on the tenth of Tishrei, ten has a palpable association with Hashem. Not surprisingly, therefore, do we find that the number of *makkos* with which the Egyptians were punished, was ten. It fits the pattern perfectly.

In much the same way as a concentrated multi-vitamin drink can provide a variety of benefits, so the ten plagues encompassed several goals. On one hand, they provided a welcome respite to the Jewish People from the unrelenting slavery. At the same time, each plague was a measure-for-measure punishment to the cruel taskmasters for their individual aspects of cruelty. Supreme amongst the purpose of the plagues were the mighty lessons –

---

1. Rabbi Yehuda ben Betzalel Loew – sixteenth-century brilliant Torah scholar in Prague.

relevant to the Egyptians and the Jews and to all posterity – of absolute knowledge of Hashem's existence, involvement in every detail of human endeavor, and unlimited potential.

In the Haggadah that we read on Pesach, Rabbi Yehuda grouped the ten plagues by their initials, דצ"ך עד"ש באח"ב. The reason that Rabbi Yehuda decided to divide the plagues into these groups was not simply to aid our memory. We do not find similar mnemonics for the twelve months of the year or the twelve tribes. What special merit did the plagues possess to be chosen? The reason is that each group had a powerful, yet totally distinct, purpose.

Any type of grouping or number pattern indicates thought, purpose, and design. In the Torah's law of returning a lost article, the Gemara (*Bava Metzia* 25b) discusses what precisely constitutes an identifiable pattern that would indicate that coins found lying on the ground were not randomly dropped, but rather placed there with thought and design. The conclusion is that if you find three coins, two lying beside each other with the third resting across the other two, the law is that you cannot keep those coins. The pattern is a strong indication that the coins were placed there purposely. If that logic prevails with one single group of three, how much more so with three consecutive groups, each which reveals a distinct pattern. It was to emphasize that distinct pattern, thought, and design apparent in the ten plagues that prompted Rabbi Yehuda to arrange his mnemonic. When we attend the Seder each year, we can never forget the three groups.

The Malbim, in his commentary to the Torah (*Shemos* 7:14), explains the pattern of each group of plagues in detail. In all three groups, the pattern is repeated. Each of the three sections was heralded with a very specific policy statement, in which the theme and purpose of that particular group was clearly enunciated.

In each group, the warning of the first plague was given first thing in the morning, outside the palace at the riverside, in order to repudiate Pharaoh's claim of divinity. (The *Midrash Tanchuma* in *Bereishis* 47:10 explains that when Yaakov met Pharaoh for the first time, he blessed the Egyptian monarch that the Nile River would overflow its banks when he approached – they would literally rise to meet him. That phenomenon allowed the Pharaohs to claim supernatural powers bordering on the divine, that even the mighty Nile, longest river in the world and the lifeline of Egypt, was subservient to them.) The warning of the second plague in each group was delivered to Pharaoh in his palace at midday, when Pharaoh sat on his throne, surrounded by his royal court. The chilling tones of dire warning echoed for all to hear.

After the clear warnings of the first two plagues in each group, the third would be delivered without warning. After two unheeded cautions came the punishment. Hence, the plagues of lice, boils, and darkness fell upon the Egyptians with no opportunity for them to protect or prepare themselves.

Pharaoh, the Egyptian mouthpiece that denied Hashem (*"Who is Hashem that I shall heed His voice to send out Israel – I do not know Hashem nor will I send out Israel"* [*Shemos* 5:2]) Who created the world with ten utterances, received his just desserts and re-education in ten plagues.

Let us now examine each of the *makkos* in closer detail, in order to gain the full *yediah* from them all. That, after all, was their true purpose. As important as the plagues were to the Egyptians, both in terms of punishment, and an opportunity to gain knowledge of Hashem (a reward for their initial hospitality to the family of Yaakov), the primary beneficiaries of the powerful lessons of the plagues were the Jewish People, who for all time would be enjoined to remember the ten plagues. It is the Jewish People who are G-d's emissaries in the world[2] and it is the Jewish People who have to be cognizant of the great and powerful *yediah* contained in the plagues. Our destiny depends on it. We have to be clear.

---

2. *You are My witnesses – the word of Hashem – and My servant whom I have chosen* (*Yeshayahu* 43:10).

TEN

Expert Opposition

Group One: דצ"ך – *dam, tzefardei'a, kinnim*. There is no knowledge more vital than knowledge of G-d. With it, life is worth living; without it, life is meaningless. To the Pharaoh who denied any knowledge of Hashem came the mighty pronouncement, *Through this you shall know that I am Hashem...* (Shemos 7:17). G-d is set to prove His existence. To all the millions who grope in the darkness, wondering, wishing that they had some solid proof on which they could pin their belief, comes this clear, unequivocal clarion call – "Through this you will know, with solid certainty, a certainty that will dispel all doubt and equivocation, now and for always, that Hashem exists." By the end of this group of plagues, the Egyptian magicians, expert in all areas of the occult, would admit defeat and declare to the world, *"This is a finger of G-d."* The proof had been given.

An extremely important point needs to be elucidated. The plague of blood was a mighty plague. The River Nile was the lifeline of all Egypt. It was their source of water. No wonder that Pharaoh was keen to make believe that the river was subservient to him. To change all the clear life-giving water of the world's longest river into thick, lifeless, turgid, coagulating blood that would kill the fish and would affect not only the river, but all canals, reservoirs, and pools, even water in wood and stone containers, was massive in its scope. It was a devastating blow to the Egyptians – everyone needs water – and a clear demonstration of Divine presence and power. But the Egyptian magicians were somehow able to replicate the plague, to some small degree; either by the power of illusion or magical incantation. However they did it, the very fact that the plague could be copied – albeit in a make-believe and limited manner – gave the petulant king the escape that he so desperately sought. If the purpose of the *makkah* was to give absolute proof of Hashem's existence, why did Hashem have to choose a plague that could be replicated by the magicians, and thus dull the effect? Hashem, by definition, is all-powerful, and is not short of plagues that would have been beyond the necromancer's ability to copy, even to any small degree; why then choose blood?

The very same question can be posed about the second plague, frogs. This plague was also a mighty manifestation of Hashem's existence. All boundaries of Egypt were swamped with these croaking amphibians; nowhere was frog-free. Even in the hallowed, fiercely guarded palace of Pharaoh, in his bedroom and his very holy, don't-you-dare-touch-it bed; everyone's homes, cooking utensils, even in the ovens (frogs hate heat, and love damp), the incessantly cacophonous croaking reptiles swarmed. It was unprecedented and massive. You would know that there was a huge Force responsible for this relentless, heaving, croaking avalanche. You would know that there was a G-d. Why then did Hashem again choose a plague that the Egyptian magicians could, in some way, replicate? Whether it was with magical incantations, or plastic inflatable frogs, the fact that they were able to somehow produce something that passed as a frog gave Pharaoh his second reprieve. Why not choose a different plague that would be equally impressive, produce the desired result, and be immune to the magicians' skills? *Is anything beyond Hashem?* (*Bereishis* 18:14).

Why was it necessary to wait until the third plague in the series, lice, which, despite their best efforts, the magicians were unable to replicate in any manner, to elicit from their unwilling mouths the words the world was waiting to hear, *"It is a finger of G-d!"* Since this admission was the purpose of the three-plague demonstration, was it not a shame to wait until practically the very end before the affirmation could be obtained?

I heard this question from my *rebbi*, Rav Mattisyahu Salomon *shlit"a*, who quoted his own *rebbi*, Rav Elya Lopian *zt"l*, who posed the question, and gave this remarkable answer which I will explain with a parable:

Suppose that a group of migrant workers come to *beis din* and request conversion forms because of their love of gefilte fish. No one would become too excited. If, however, the President of the Royal Society of Advanced Scientific Research came to *beis din* seeking conversion based on his solid conviction that there is none but Hashem, the impact and repercussions of that request would be profound; and the *kiddush Hashem* – enormous.

Of all the ancient civilizations, few are as rich in relics, artifacts, and buildings as the Egyptians. The mighty pyramids bear silent but articulate witness to the extent of the building skills, techniques, transport systems, and mathematical calculations of the early Egyptians. They were anything but primitive, and possessed areas of expertise that even to the contemporary observer are remarkable. These were the people who Hashem wished to convince of His existence. These were the members of the Opposition. Imagine that Hashem would have chosen three plagues which the Egyptian magicians would have not been able to replicate. Then there might have been a danger. We, living more than three thousand years later, could have thought, "Who were the people who so long ago admitted the existence of G-d? They must have been primitives, like natives in the African jungle, who, if you show them a cigarette lighter, will fall to your feet and declare you their Big Chief because you have made fire come from your fingers."

"Absolutely not," says Hashem. The Torah declares that they had the ability – somehow – to produce blood and frogs. *You* cannot turn water into sticky blood; *you* cannot produce frogs. They could. Look at the pyramids. Look at their knowledge. Look at their magicians. They were clever men. They were the scientists of their age. They were sophisticated and knowledgeable. And it was these people – the very people who knew all about magic – who begrudgingly but honestly admitted the existence of Hashem.

To achieve maximum *kiddush Hashem*, it was required that centuries later, we should know just how knowledgeable and capable the erstwhile and eventual supporters were who would declare, *"This is a finger of G-d."*

ELEVEN

Divine Intervention

Group Two: ערד"ש – *arov, dever, shechin*. After establishing the existence of Hashem, the next vital lesson was that Hashem is involved in every detail of life. There might be those who think that, though Hashem exists, He cannot possibly be interested in the mundane minutiae of everyday life. Nothing could be further from the truth. Moshe confronted Pharaoh at the commencement of the second group of *makkos* to warn him that failure to release his Jewish slaves will result in swarms of wild animals invading the palace, the homes, the very ground on which the Egyptians stood. *And on that day, I shall set apart the land of Goshen upon which My people stands – that area of Egypt will be immune to the wild animals – so that you will know that I am Hashem in the midst of the land* (*Shemos* 8:18).

No human agency can control the precise movements of animals, whom they will attack and whom not. Imagine that a circus comes to town, complete with ferocious animals in their metal cages. A calamity occurs – the lions and tigers break out of their cages and are now freely roaming along the avenue, spreading terror, panic, and consternation. The mayor of the town, in a brave attempt to restore calm, cruises down the street in his mayoral jeep, and announces, "Citizens of my town – fear not! There is no

Divine Intervention

danger! The lions and tigers are democratic animals, and anyone who voted Democrat in the last election will be safe. The animals will only attack Republicans!" Brave, but futile words. No human agency can control whom the animals will attack, or in which area they will encroach. A promise, in advance, guaranteeing the safety of a particular group of people can only be made by the Creator Who is also the Supreme Controller.

The second plague – the second witness of the great principle of Hashem's control – was an animal epidemic. Faithfully following the previous pattern, Moshe was commanded to appear in Pharaoh's palace and warn him that continued refusal to release his slaves would result in the death of his livestock. All animals within the borders of Egypt – horses, donkeys, camels, cattle – would perish. The sole survivors would be the livestock owned by Jewish people. A precise timescale was given, stating that the plague would begin the following day. Exactly as promised, the plague struck the next day, devastating Egyptian-owned livestock, while not a single animal owned by a Jew was affected. The Ramban explains that the miracle was accentuated by the fact that the Egyptians worshipped animals and detested sheep-herders. Consequently, they concentrated most of their own livestock in Goshen, where they mingled with Jewish-owned animals. Thus, the survival of Jewish-owned flocks – which shared the pasture, water, and air of Egyptian livestock – was an undeniable miracle.

Any human being could never, and would never utter such a precise prediction. At best, he would forecast some vague prospect or foreboding, including sufficient margin of error for any eventuality. "Tomorrow's weather is likely to be changeable with a possibility of showers," "Vote for me for a more prosperous and secure future." Here, Pharaoh was told in clear and unequivocal language: *Not a single animal belonging to the Children of Israel will die* (*Shemos* 9:5). And do not imagine that Pharaoh, desperate to maintain his policy of denial, did not check out the prediction. *Pharaoh sent, and behold, of the livestock of Israel not even one had died* (ibid. 9:7). This was an absolute detailed promise, precisely delivered as spoken, with not a single solitary exception. That is knowledge. *So that you will* know *that I am Hashem in the midst of the land* (ibid. 8:18).

We are told to remember *Yetzias Mitzrayim* every single day of our lives (*Devarim* 16:3). All the lessons learned from that momentous period in our history are not simply historic. They are truths that apply, without exception, for all times; G-d is aware of everything that transpires in every aspect of everyone's lives, every action, every thought. He manipulates and orchestrates our lives in reaction to our behavior.

Listen to a story of Divine interaction which is probably the least dramatic story ever told – yet typical of thousands of similar stories that everyone can tell. On a Thursday morning in October 1999, a man went to immerse some household items in the *keilim mikvah* in the Gateshead Shul. Because of the proximity of the *keilim mikvah* to the men's *mikvah*, there are frequently hats placed on the cover over the *mikvah*. The gentleman involved removed a hat, placed it to one side, and proceeded with the dipping process.

At the same time, the owner of the hat exited the men's *mikvah* and looked for his hat. Noticing it to the side of the busy individual dipping dishes, he picked it up with a look of intense displeasure on his face. His precious hat had been unceremoniously placed in a puddle of water lying on the surface. The owner shook off the water from his hat accompanied by profuse apologies from the dipper, who had not noticed the puddle of water in which the hat had been placed. Later that day, the man who had caused the minor grief was walking to Minchah when suddenly a gust of wind came and blew his hat off, depositing it unceremoniously into a puddle of water. Causing minor grief. The man shook the water off the rim, and began thinking. Who knew of the initial incident? Who can create and control a freak gust of wind – on the same day? Who knew about the puddle on the road? No action is too small to cause a reaction, no incident or word is too insignificant to warrant a consequence. Nothing is ignored or forgotten – *So that you will know that I am Hashem in the midst of the land.*

TWELVE

A Closer Look at Divine Control

What would you say about the following situation? We'll describe it in the words of the protagonist: "One bright morning, I was driving along a side road, approaching a main road. Coming toward me slowly down the main road was a car driven by a student-driver. As I approached the junction, I applied my foot to the brake in order to stop and allow the student-driver to pass. For some inexplicable reason, and perhaps for the very first time ever, my foot accidentally pressed on the accelerator, causing my car to shoot out into the main road. A look of shock and horror crossed the face of the other driver. He swerved and I quickly pressed the correct pedal and stopped my car in time to avert a collision. The poor driver was shaken, and I mouthed sincere apologies, severely shame-faced.

"Later on the same day, I was driving home from Minchah along that same main road. As I was driving along, minding my own business, a car suddenly pulled out from a parked position at the side of the road just in front of me, and for some inexplicable reason, began pulling into the center of the road. I received the shock of my life; I was convinced I would collide with him, and quickly swerved. At the last moment, he noticed me and stopped, shame-faced. Collision averted. Upon reflection, I realized that every single detail of the two incidents were identical. The near miss, the shock involved, the same street, the same day – nothing is too insignificant, too trivial, to escape the attention and scrutiny of Hashem."

This mighty principle, that Hashem is actively involved in all details of the world, was clearly demonstrated in the second group of plagues. But it does not end there. The knowledge that Hashem has of events transpiring on earth is not passive or inactive. Every single action has a reaction. Every single deed has a consequence. In the Thirteen Principles of Faith enunciated by the Rambam, the statement expressing our belief that Hashem knows all the deeds and thoughts of human beings is followed by our acceptance of the fact that Hashem rewards those who observe His commandments, and punishes those who violate His commandments. There is no one, without exception, who cannot discern Hashem in his own life, on the basis of, *According to the measure with which one measures out his actions, they (the Heavenly Tribunal) measure for him in return.* What you do to others, others will do to you. It is not arbitrary. It is not haphazard. It is precise, measured, and directed by Hashem.

Another story that demonstrates this: There was a family in Gateshead who was having a *simchah*, and one family member's parents were coming from out of town to attend. Chaim, an acquaintance, asked the family member if he knew who was picking up his parents from the station. The gentleman, surprisingly, showed no interest, and said he had no idea! Chaim felt his attitude was somewhat lacking, so he went himself to collect them, although he was not related. A short time later, traveling down to London by train, Chaim spied this person on the same train. He was visiting his family in London. When they arrived at the station in London, who was there to meet him? No one. He was alone, friendless and unrecognized. Chaim, on the other hand, was not only picked up at the station, but at each stage of the evening's subsequent traveling, he received an abundance of offers for rides.

Everyone can, and should, relate their own stories. They do not have to be dramatic. But they show very clearly, very demonstrably, and very convincingly, the presence of Hashem in our lives. This realization enables us all to avoid trouble and to enjoy a peaceful and happy life. If one causes grief needlessly to someone, he will eventually be the recipient of grief in like measure. *Hillel saw a skull floating on the water. He said to it, "Because you drowned others, they drowned you; and those who drowned you will drown eventually"* (*Pirkei Avos* 2:7). Innumerable examples of "measure for measure" are to be found in the Torah. Yaakov gained his father's blessing through subterfuge (albeit at his mother's instruction); his chosen wife, Rochel, was denied to him through Lavan's subterfuge. Yaakov was absent from his father for twenty-two years; his son Yosef was absent from his home for twenty-two years. Yosef made very specific allegations against his brothers' behavior; each of these allegations rebounded precisely onto Yosef. It is indeed a list without end, for it is a principle with which Hashem runs the world: If you perform a kindness to someone, a kindness will be done to you. This formula is so reliable, that a certain representative of a Torah institution makes sure to perform a significant kindness to someone before asking a benefactor for a significant sum. Hashem directs operations. Doing people favors, making people happy, giving compliments, smiling and greeting people pleasantly, thinking of something positive to say to people, are the greatest guarantee of reciprocal behavior.

But what about when we do *not* see a corresponding reaction to an action?

The first thing to bear in mind is that the timescale of *middah k'neged middah* is not always immediate. We find that Mordechai cried *a loud and bitter cry* (Esther 4:1) and we are taught that it is a result of Yaakov causing Eisav to cry *an exceedingly great and bitter cry* (Bereishis 27:34). Hashem's vigilance is constant and unerring, but the timescale can span centuries.

But there is another caveat to this principle. A *mohel* causes a little baby much pain and discomfort. The little child cries and cries! Does the *mohel* receive pain for the pain caused? An emissary of a *beis din* has to administer thirty-nine lashes. This is his unpleasant task, one that causes much suffering. Does it make him deserving of punishment? Avraham our forefather sent away his very own son Yishmael from his home. The boy was not well, and we can imagine that much anguish was caused by the expulsion. Did Avraham suffer measure for measure as a result?

It is essential to know that within the principle of "measure for measure" is a qualification that if the grief or pain was mandated by Hashem, then no reciprocal pain will visit the one who administrated the pain. The *mohel*, the *beis din* employee, and Avraham Avinu were all fulfilling Hashem's command, in which case there is no retribution. In the same way that a *shochet*, who spends his day killing cows, sheep, and chickens, will not fear that he might suffer the same fate, or the person cutting the grass will not fear an attack from a giant grass-cutter, similarly, someone who has to cause pain, discomfort, or disappointment, but does so in order to discharge an obligation, can do so with equanimity if he is performing the wish of Hashem.

This special characteristic in the law of "measure for measure" is the strongest indication that it emanates directly from Hashem. It is neither all-embracing nor is it haphazard, but under the sole control of the Supreme Arbitrator – *So that you will know that I am Hashem in the midst of the land.*

THIRTEEN
Divine Control in History

In the same way that Divine control is demonstrated by the sequence of events in an individual's life, so it is demonstrated in an even greater manner in the existence of the Jewish People as a whole. Politicians, whose primary ambition is to remain in their positions of power, are keen to predict that adhering to a particular economic plan will produce prosperity. More work, greater income, and increased productivity will produce economic buoyancy. In an economic downturn, voters will be required to endure increased taxation with the assurance that this will assist the climb toward recovery. All is predictable, logical, and consistent with good housekeeping and common sense.

If, however, predictions are made connecting the prosperity of a nation, linking that economic buoyancy to spiritual activities, then all logic evaporates and disappears. Take an example: Imagine that the Prime Minister of England would give advance warning of an important announcement to be made in the Houses of Parliament. At the specified time, the Prime Minister would stand up, address the crowded benches with a serious demeanor, and say, "I have asked you to be gathered here today to listen to an announcement of the greatest significance. I am requesting –

and indeed intend to legislate – that from the first day of October next year, and for the duration of a full year, all manufacturing activities in this country must cease. That includes all areas of industry: ship-building; coal mining; steel production; car manufacturing; all machinery manufacture, maintenance, and repair. Every aspect of productivity, from aviation to producing zippers, must cease for this entire year. Nothing will be made, nothing will be exported. All workshops, factories, and production lines will remain shut down for the entire period. It will be a time of total closure. And, I have to tell you all, the promise of the greatest prosperity, or absolute financial ruin, depends on the nation's compliance with these laws. If the nation is obedient and ceases from all productivity, then England will be healthy, wealthy, prosperous, and affluent. If, however, the nation decides to disobey this edict and continue to produce, allowing factories to remain open, then economic ruin is assured. Famine and drought will follow – and worse still – the Russians, aided by the North Koreans, will invade our country, remove us forcibly into bitter exile, and our beloved green and pleasant land will be barren and bereft, devoid of all vegetation and Englishmen. That, gentlemen, is all I have to say. I have spoken."

Several things will then happen, in fast sequence. Pandemonium would ensue. The members of the opposition would not believe their luck. The Prime Minister would have handed them the reins of government on a plate. He would remain in power just long enough to fill his cardboard box with the contents of his office desk, chocolate biscuits and all, and exit the stage of power and privilege with many years of retirement ahead of him to write his sorry memoirs. The poor members of the Prime Minister's party will bury their heads in their hands. The poor man had gone mad. The strains of leadership must have affected the balance of his mind. Imagine; don't work and prosperity will follow. Do work and the Russians will invade! The whole idea is totally preposterous.

Now, look in the Torah and you will see that that which has been described above is but a contemporary analogy of the law of *shemittah*, in which all agricultural activity ceases in the seventh year. A country surrounded by enemies, whose source of sustenance is the food they grow, is commanded to terminate that activity for a whole year. Nothing is planted, nothing grows, nothing is harvested, the surrounding enemies will not run to the Jews' assistance; it is a year of Shabbos to Hashem (*Vayikra* 25:4). Then the prediction. Clearly written (ibid. 26). If you faithfully observe the laws of cessation of work in the seventh year, the rains will come, prosperity and peace will benefit all, and the bountiful produce of previous years' abundant harvests will provide ample nourishment both during and after the seventh year. Failure to observe the laws will result in the severest of punishments, pestilence, poverty, illness, invasion of enemies, and eventual exile. The Land of Israel, which was deprived of its rest while the Jewish people resided there, will receive its rest during the years of desolation, when the defeated Jews will be exiled to the lands of their enemies. Such predictions are impossible to make; impossible for anyone but Hashem, that is.

Every Jewish male over the age of thirteen wears *tefillin* six days a week. One of the four paragraphs written on the parchment, residing both in the hand and head *tefillin*, is the second paragraph of Shema. Taken from the Torah (*Devarim* 11:13-21), the verses describe the Jewish People's responsibility to observe G-d's commandments and the clearly defined consequences of reward and punishment. Ideally, *tefillin* are meant to be worn throughout the day. That means that every Jewish man carries on his head and arm written testimony of the consequences of his own actions, and those of his people. It is a fact we may never forget, one described in the Torah again and again in great detail. It lives in the present, and we see it clearly in our history.

Hashem wants us to know of His existence. Linking observance of religious precepts to the destiny of a nation, with both positive and negative repercussions which are clearly defined in precise detail, transcends logic. It is, however, the strongest and clearest indication that a Divine hand controls the fate of all nations, and the Jewish People in particular.

FOURTEEN
The Nature of the Unnatural

Group Three: באח"ב – *barad, arbeh, choshech, bechoros.* The word nature by definition means a series of preset laws by which this world operates. The purpose of the last set of plagues was to demonstrate that Hashem, Who creates those laws, has the ability to change and override those laws at will. This group, like the previous two, began with Moshe meeting Pharaoh early in the morning and delivering a policy statement. But there was one difference. Whereas in the first two groups, Moshe was commanded to meet Pharaoh at the water, at this juncture, Pharaoh had learned his lesson and was reluctant to make his customary watery rendezvous. Instead, he wanted to leave his palace early in the morning to an undisclosed location, where he could be sure not to meet Moshe. For that reason, Moshe was commanded to appear early in the day at the palace, and meet the startled Pharaoh as he made his exit.

The message issued by Hashem was clear. *For this time, I shall send all My plagues against your heart and upon your servants, and your people, so that you shall know that there is none like Me in all the world* (*Shemos* 9:14). After Hashem has proven that He exists, and that His control extends to every smallest detail, Hashem wishes us to know that there is nothing beyond His capability. The words that were said to Avraham, *Is anything beyond Hashem?* (*Bereishis* 18:14), would now be illustrated in their full grandeur.

The first plague in this final series was the devastating *makkah* of hail. One might assume that in the hot Mediterranean climate of Egypt, hail – pallets of frozen rain, falling in showers – was not a common phenomenon. But it could certainly happen. If it can snow in Jerusalem, it can hail in Egypt. This, however, was no regular hail. *There was hail, and fire flaming amid the hail* (*Shemos* 9:24). This was a miracle within a miracle. Firstly, the fire shot downward, though fire usually rises; secondly, the fire and water functioned in unison. Everyone knows that fire evaporates water, and water extinguishes fire. They are mutually destructive. Yet here, to demonstrate the power of Hashem, the regular rules of nature were transcended. The one who makes the rules can break the rules.

The Malbim, quoting sources in the Midrash, states that when Moshe prophesied, *Behold at this time tomorrow I shall rain a very heavy hail...* (*Shemos* 9:18), he scratched a mark on the wall indicating that at the precise moment at which the shadow of the sun would reach that point, the plague would begin. The Egyptian sorcerers, always eager to disprove Moshe's predictions, took careful note of the time. The Malbim understands that the fire that accompanied the thunder was lightning. Now, everyone knows that thunder and lightning never begin simultaneously. Lightning is perceived as a flash of light, and light travels at a speed of 186,282 miles per *second*. Practically speaking, a person sees light instantly. Sound, in stark contrast, travels through air at a far slower speed of 730 miles per *hour*, or one mile every five seconds. For that reason, if you'd wish to know how distant the lightning is during a storm, count seconds from when you see the lightning flash until you hear the thunder, divide that number by five, and you will know the distance. In Egypt, if the plague of hail would be accompanied by lightning together with thunder, then the plague should begin with lightning, followed some seconds later by the sound of thunder. The Egyptian magicians, anxiously watching that mark on the wall, would notice the delay, and delightedly declare the prophecy flawed. For that reason, the Torah states, *Hashem sent thunder and hail, and fire went earthward...* (ibid. 9:23), emphasizing that Hashem transcended the laws of nature to bring everything together, suddenly and simultaneously, at the precisely predicted moment.

Harav Avigdor Miller *zt"l*, in his commentary on *Shemos* (*A Nation Is Born*), writes, "This hail was not merely ice, but also stones, heated by the great fire among them. (In *Brachos* 54b this "hail" is compared to the hail of stones of Elgabish that fell in Yehoshua's time.) Thus, this hail was unique not only in Egypt's history, but also in the history of nations; for the uniqueness was not merely in the size of the hailstones and in the intensity and duration of the hail, but it was unequaled in the fact that these were very hot pallets of solid stone. Falling from the heights, the heated stones acquired a great velocity, so that each stone became a deadly missile that destroyed whatever it struck. The entire land became a conflagration and Pharaoh's advisers declared that Egypt was lost."

In addition to Hashem demonstrating His dominion over nature, the Torah mentions that in this plague, just like the previous set, the Divine control was absolute. *Only in the land of Goshen, where the children of Israel were, there was no hail* (ibid. 9:26).

Hashem's ability to manipulate nature at His command was further demonstrated by the eighth plague, the plague of locusts. This catastrophe, unprecedented in its ferocity, would destroy the remnants of the produce that the hail had left over. Moshe, together with Aharon, came to Pharaoh's palace and issued the clear and unequivocal warning: if he would continue to stubbornly refuse to release the Jewish People, the next day would see a dense swarm of locusts enter the country, covering the entire surface, effectively concealing any sight of the land. Amazingly, in an unprecedented display of Divine control, the locust swarm would adhere religiously to the border, without a single locust crossing the threshold. Due to this accuracy, many border disputes involving Egypt and its neighbors were resolved (*Midrash Rabbah*). In a detailed and frightening prophecy, Pharaoh was told clearly that the locusts would consume every remnant of vegetation left by the hail, and they would fill every single Egyptian house (again emphasizing the total exclusion of Jewish houses) in a density and intensity that had never been seen in all Egyptian history.

Given the accuracy of the predictions in the preceding plagues, the terrifying prospect of the devastation of the land so alarmed the Egyptian ministers that they begged Pharaoh to

The Nature of the Unnatural

end his obduracy and release the Jews. True to form, Pharaoh refused to be humbled, and precisely as foretold, the swarm swept into the country. The locust not only harassed the Egyptians in the fields, but also disrupted their homes. The foodstuffs in the pantries and kitchens were infested by the voracious flying insects, and all vegetables and grain were devoured. The limitless power of Hashem was proven by the clear statement that entirely as predicted, this was the most severe locust swarm ever to inflict Egypt, either before or after (*Shemos* 10:14). Pharaoh, with customary contrition while suffering the plague, begged Moshe to entreat Hashem and remove the flying death. At Hashem's direction, the east wind that blew the locusts into Egypt was changed to a westerly wind which blew them out again, without a single locust, alive, dead, or pickled, remaining in the land. The lifeless land resembled a post-nuclear Hiroshima landscape, with the absolutely barren and desolate terrain giving graphic evidence of the fulfillment of the Divine decree.

Consistent with the pattern that the third plague in each series came without warning, the next plague came with the suddenness of a blackout. At Hashem's command, from one second to the next, darkness descended on Egypt. For a period of six days, the Egyptians were bathed in blackness. No light, no sight penetrated the inky and opaque gloom. The six days were divided into two periods, one worse than the other. For the first three days, all was black, without a glimmer to brighten the somber murkiness. But at least they could move. Groping, hoping they would not injure themselves, they stumbled along, arms outstretched, shrouded in an impenetrable obscurity. But they could at least function. During the second three days, the darkness became tangible. It was a thick solidified darkness that prevented the Egyptians from moving. Frozen in grotesque postures, like nightmarish statues, the Egyptians remained rooted to their place, unable to move a finger or lift an eyelid. In an incredible contrast, the Jewish People were bathed in light. The Torah states, *No man could see his brother, nor could anyone rise from his place for a three-day period, but for all the Children of Israel, there was light in their dwellings.* The commentators note the word "dwellings" rather than the usual term "Goshen" to indicate that even when the Jews entered the dwellings of the Egyptians, they experienced full daylight at the same time that the Egyptians were immobilized in their sightlessness. Nothing could more eloquently illustrate that it is Hashem Who "forms light and creates darkness" than this unprecedented phenomenon of light and darkness occurring in complete contrast – simultaneously.

The hail, the locusts, and finally, the darkness, vividly proved to the Egyptians, and to ourselves, that indeed, *...you shall know that there is none like Me in all the world* (ibid. 9:14). The same nature that is the regular directive of Hashem can be turned on its head at Hashem's command. Nature and Unnatural has a single source – Hashem.

FIFTEEN
The Lock Is Sprung

The tenth and final plague was different than all its predecessors. Before Moshe had even left Midyan, he was informed in a prophecy that the initial nine plagues would not effect the release of the enslaved nation. *When you go to return to Egypt, see all the wonders that I have put in your hand and perform them before Pharaoh; but I shall strengthen his heart, and he will not send out the people* (ibid. 4:21). Those nine plagues were lessons for the Egyptians and the Jewish People forever that there is a G-d Who controls and manipulates all. That spectrum of powerful proofs is remembered every single day: *That you may remember the day of your departure from the land of Egypt all the days of your life* (Devarim 16:3), and formed the living proof that the Jewish People could refer to when they heard Hashem communicate with them at Mount Sinai, *I am Hashem, Who has taken you out of the land of Egypt, from the House of Slavery* (Shemos 20:1).

It was at that time in Midyan that Moshe was told that the killing of the Egyptian firstborn would unlock the mighty impenetrable prison doors and finally release the Jewish People. *You shall say to Pharaoh, "So says Hashem, My firstborn son is Israel. So I say to you, send out My son that he may serve Me – but you have refused to send him out; behold I shall kill your firstborn son."* In fulfillment of that promise, Moshe was now commanded to appear to Pharaoh one final time and inform him that at midnight every firstborn in the land of Egypt will die, from the firstborn of Pharaoh who sits on the throne, to the firstborn of the maidservant who is behind the millstone, and all the firstborn animals (*Shemos* 11:4-8). The result of this terrible blow was precisely predicted. *There shall be a great outcry in the entire land of Egypt, such as there has never been, and such as there shall never be again. But against all the Children of Israel, no dog shall whet its tongue, against neither man nor animal, so that you shall know that Hashem has differentiated between Egypt and Israel. Then all those servants of yours will come down to Me and bow to Me, saying, "Leave – you and the entire people that follows you"* (ibid. 11:1).

Just like the final movement of a symphony incorporates all the features of the previous movements, so did the final plague of the killing of the firstborn contain aspects of the three powerful lessons of the three sets of plagues, climaxing in a grand finale that sprung the lock of the Egyptian servitude. An act of retribution against the Egyptians, who had so persecuted the "firstborn" of Hashem, in which every Egyptian firstborn would perish at a precisely predicted moment, in a manner that no Egyptian house would be excluded, is an unprecedented act of G-d that no one could ever replicate. The total exclusion of the Jewish nation from this country-wide devastation was the clearest evidence that Hashem exercises complete control over His creation. And the very nature of this final plague, that selected members of every single Egyptian family would suddenly die, without any prior illness or infirmity, was a dramatic and overwhelming illustration of Hashem's unlimited capability.

As a direct result of this cataclysmic event, the Jewish people would forever need to show gratitude, both for our firstborn's salvation, and for the Exodus that resulted from this final plague. *And it shall be when your son will ask you at some future time, "What is this?" you shall say to him, "With a strong hand Hashem removed us from Egypt, from the House of Bondage. And it happened when Pharaoh stubbornly refused to send us out, that Hashem killed all the firstborns in the land of Egypt, from the firstborn of man to the firstborn of animals. Therefore, I offer to Hashem all male first issue of the womb, and I shall redeem all the firstborn of my sons"* (ibid. 13:14-15).

As the Jews engaged in the mitzvos of their very first *korban Pesach*, their hearts clinging to Hashem for His protection, all around them the plague spread despair and panic like a contagion through the land. It was both a frightening and thrilling moment for them. In front of their eyes, they saw how observance of Hashem's commands guarantees life, and how the stubborn deniers are destined for destruction. The remembrance of the final plague, during which the Jewish People actively participated in the special mitzvos just prior to their departure from Egypt, is re-enacted every year, so that the impact and importance of that historic event should never fade.

In each generation a person is obligated to look at himself as though he personally departed from Egypt (*Pesachim* 116b). And know, with clear and unequivocal knowledge, that Hashem exists, that He controls to the finest detail, and that His potential and capability is unlimited.

SIXTEEN

The Key to Popularity

Something happened just prior to the Exodus that, according to authoritative opinion, was the greatest wonder of them all. While Moshe was still in Midyan, he was told by Hashem of the impending plagues that would afflict the Egyptians, and Pharaoh's obduracy in refusing to release the Jews. Then, immediately, he was told something else. *Each woman shall request from her neighbor and from the one who lives in her house, silver vessels, golden vessels, and garments* (Shemos 3:22). This instruction is repeated twice more, to include the men having to do the same. The command was not forgotten. On the very night of departure, when the Egyptians were recoiling from the devastation of the plague of the firstborn, *The children of Israel carried out the word of Moshe – they requested from the Egyptians silver vessels, gold vessels, and garments* (ibid. 12:35).

Why was this so amazing? My *rebbi*, Harav Mattisyahu Salomon *shlit"a*, explains that we have to visualize the situation. In the space of one year, Egypt had been completely devastated. The country that epitomized wealth, power, and prosperity; the bread-basket of the entire world; the mightiest empire, had been transformed into a drab sad land of pestilence and poverty. Reeling from ten successive catastrophes which had destroyed the economy, decimated the population, and left the survivors depressed, defeated, and dejected, they look at the Jews – the cause of their downfall – with unmitigated animosity. Finally, the Jews are leaving. But just prior to their departure, they have one final task to perform: to ask their Egyptian neighbors for all their money. Imagine yourself as an Egyptian – how would you react? Here is the man, whom you see as responsible for all your troubles and misery, quietly standing at the door, calmly requesting the one thing of value still remaining. "Hello – we're going now – could you please give me all your silver and gold? Oh, and by the way, could I have your precious clothes also?" The normal reaction would have been anger and fury. What insolence, what a nerve! The request should have triggered an angry and violent response, at the very least. Instead, what do we see? *Hashem gave the people favor in the eyes of the Egyptians and they granted their request – so they emptied Egypt* (ibid. 12:36).

This was the mightiest miracle. Not only did Hashem control water, amphibious animals, tiny creatures, large animals, animal sickness, human sickness, climate, winged creatures, light and darkness, life itself – but Hashem could control minds. A mind that should revile and hate could be transformed into a mind, an attitude, of benevolence and kindness. "Sure you can have all my money. Here – don't forget the gold – come, my beloved Jewish neighbor, let me help you pack!"

It is interesting and important to know that there are two other parallels of this phenomenon of Hashem controlling the minds of men in a spectacular manner. Earlier in the Torah, we read how Pharaoh was sorely troubled by the dreams of the seven cows, fat and thin, followed by the seven ears of grain, fulsome and stricken. His mind was perturbed, and none of the interpretations of the resident magicians and soothsayers calmed his frazzled nerves. His butler suddenly remembered the Jewish slave who was his fellow prisoner, who had successfully explained his own and his late friend – the lamented baker's – dream. The butler, while wishing to ingratiate himself to Pharaoh by introducing Yosef, was keen to emphasize that this lad had three significant disadvantages. He was young and inexperienced, a slave, and a Jew. No doubt, even if he would successfully interpret the dreams, he would safely be re-incarcerated to his former dungeon.

Yosef was duly summoned and was rushed to Pharaoh. Now consider: if you would have been advising Yosef on the correct manner, demeanor, and attitude to adopt in order to best maximize his chances of gaining favor and freedom, you would have told him to show deference and humility to the Mighty Monarch, to speak only when requested to do so, and under no circumstances to contradict anything the king said. To contradict the king is to anger the king, and an angry Pharaoh is a dangerous Pharaoh. The Royal Baker could attest to that.

Now witness what happened. Pharaoh began the conversation. *"I dreamt a dream, but no one can interpret it. Now, I have heard it said of you that you can comprehend a dream to interpret it."* According to your sage advice, given in full compliance with the rules of how to win friends and influence kings, Yosef should have modestly smiled, and softly and sweetly said, "Your Majesty is too kind. I do try my best." Instead, Yosef answered in a loud and defiant rebuttal. *"That is beyond me. It is G-d Who will respond with Pharaoh's welfare"* (ibid. 41:15-16). You, the hapless adviser, would be burying your head in your hands, waiting for the ominous reaction of an enraged Pharaoh to this unprecedented insolence. Instead, surprisingly, Pharaoh seems oblivious and continues to relate both dreams. At the end of the recitation, Yosef gives his considered verdict, again quoting G-d as the origin of the dreams. He speaks of the seven years of plenty, followed by the seven years of famine. What happens then is beyond belief. Completely unbidden, with absolute confidence, Yosef advises Pharaoh on the correct strategy that will ensure that the land of Egypt stores the huge surplus of produce judiciously, in order to remain impervious to the ravages of the ensuing famine. Instead of Pharaoh and his officers listening aghast to the unprecedented behavior of this precocious Jewish slave and reacting with rage and fury, the very opposite happens. *The matter appeared good in Pharaoh's eyes and in the eyes of all his servants. "Could we find another like him – a man in whom is the spirit of G-d?"* (ibid. 41:37-38).

To add wonder to wonders, Pharaoh then appoints Yosef as the man in charge of the whole operation, elevates him to Viceroy of Egypt, a position second only to Pharaoh himself. From prisoner to prime minister in ten minutes! To say that this event was unprecedented is to understate the case. Never in a million years would anyone have imagined such a course of events. The G-d Who transformed the minds of the Egyptians from cruel to benign in order to fulfill the promise of leaving Egypt with great wealth, was the G-d Who sprinkled the mind of the mighty monarch and his ambitious selfish officers with the milk of human kindness to enable Yosef to attain the pivotal position necessary for his vital role in the history of the Jewish People.

The third example of this phenomenon occurred a thousand years later in far-off Persia, when Achashveirosh was seeking a new wife to replace the late Queen Vashti. The king instructed, "Every young maiden of beautiful appearance should be gathered to Shushan the capital." The king was the type of man who considered himself something of an expert in matters of feminine beauty, and clear guidelines were given to ascertain that when each contestant would arrive for her interview, she would have received all the cosmetic preparations necessary to create a fine impression. In addition, each contestant was given whatever she requested to enhance her appeal. We can imagine that every one of those women went to great lengths to discover the king's personal preferences in style and color, in order to increase their chance of success. They all – each and every one of them – very much wanted to win the contest.

Only one woman had no interest whatsoever in the whole affair. She did not want to create a good impression, requested nothing to accompany her to the palace, and absolutely did not want to become the queen to this corpulent character. If a person wants to create a poor impression, it is very easy to do so. No smile, blank expression, a reluctance in every move and posture, a negative attitude in every nuance that cannot be disguised.

Could you imagine how a child would come to the front of the class when summoned to explain why she has not done her homework? That is how Esther made her grand entrance to the king. Add to that the fact that, according to *Chazal*, Esther had a greenish tinge, and the picture is complete. The king should have taken one look at Esther and turned away fast. Instead, amazingly, he was captivated. Hashem endowed her with a special grace, and she found favor in the eyes of the king.

This last wonder in the Exodus from Egypt is the secret of popularity. There can be every reason and likelihood for rejection and disfavor, and *Hashem Yisbarach*, Who controls the minds of men, can make Pharaoh's heart full of admiration for Yosef, the Egyptians wish to give all their money to the *Bnei Yisrael*, and Achashveirosh to be entranced by Esther. *Hashem gave the people favor.* Then, and always.

SEVENTEEN
Measure for Measure

There are two types of weddings. Although they are as different in style as day and night, from the invitation they look deceivingly similar. Both print the names of the bride and groom, parents and grandparents, location of the *chuppah*, and time of commencement. That is where the similarity ends. Although both invitations may print the same time – say 5:00 p.m. – by the first type of wedding, if you appear at the hall at the stated time, you would think you have come to the wrong location. No one is there. In vain might you search for a *chuppah*. Eventually, you may see someone dressed in Shabbos clothes and ask if this is indeed the place where the wedding is scheduled.

"Sure," will come the confident response.

"So where is the *chuppah*?"

"They're soon coming to set it up."

You will hear the word "soon" many times. *When will the* chuppah *begin... when will the bride arrive... when will they write the* kesubah... *when will the* rav *come... when will the meal begin... when will the dancing begin... when is* bentching? "Soon." Heart plummeting, you realize that you are trapped in a disorganized event, where no one is quite sure what is happening next, where no one seems to be in a hurry, where time is irrelevant. Resigned to your fate, you find a chair in the echoingly empty wedding hall, pull out your pocket-sized Chumash, and commence *shnayim mikra* with the gloomy confidence that you'll be able to finish the *parshah* more than once before the wedding begins. It's going to be a very long night.

At the opposite end of the spectrum, you will find the second type. Precisely at 5:00 p.m., with punctuality that would make the Swiss Railways envious, the groom is marched in, flanked by two fathers holding the hapless fellow in a tight grip. In quick succession, and right on time, comes the bride and her entourage. Everything is in place; the *rav*, the witnesses, the guests honored with *brachos*. At the side of the *chuppah* stands a confident young man holding the coveted list, with every name of every honoree correctly spelled, with the accurate full name of the yeshivah he represents, and his precise job description. Anyone foolish enough to arrive late – even by twenty minutes – will be sorely disappointed. The *chuppah* is being dismantled, the guests are busy demolishing the well-laid tables, and the musician is reeling in his cables.

If you stay for the dinner, you know with happy confidence that it will run on time. The bride and groom know at what time they must make their grand entry, the musicians know precisely how long the first dance will last. The speakers (if any) know in which order they will be called (before the soup, after the soup, or in the soup) and exactly how long they must speak. Every speech has been coordinated with the caterer and musician and naturally, the video operator, without which no wedding is complete, is correctly located and positioned at every stage. The men receiving *sheva brachos* will be informed in advance, and will stand in line to attention beside the top table, ready to slot into the celebrant's chair, wine, siddur and microphone at the ready. Every participant in this wedding is happy and secure in the knowledge that every detail has been thought of, coordinated, and well planned. He knows when the wedding will finish – and best of all – he may even have an early night.

The difference between the two styles is simple. One has been organized, with thought and consideration; the other is haphazard and casual. The more we see system and method in an arrangement, the more convinced we are of a grand design, whereas a chaotic, sloppy event leaves us wondering whether anyone is really in charge.

The ten plagues are a case in point. Rather than a haphazard medley of random events, there was a precise and orderly progression both in the promise given to Avraham Avinu and in their implementation.

Hashem said to Avraham, *Know with certainty that your offspring will be aliens in a land not their own – and they will serve them and they will oppress them – four hundred years. But also the nation that they will serve, I shall judge...* (Bereishis 15:13-14). Rav Samson Raphael Hirsch informs us that the servitude, as described above, will come in three stages: they will be made to feel like strangers (*geirus*), they will be enslaved (*avdus*), and they will suffer physical hurt (*inuy*). In that Divine promise, Hashem assures

Avraham that He will judge the perpetrators. Rashi comments that this judgment alludes to the ten plagues. Since Hashem's judgment is always meted out in a manner of measure for measure, we would expect that the ten plagues would reflect the three stages of the servitude. And indeed, they correspond precisely.

Firstly, a definition of terms. *Geirus*, or being made to feel like a stranger, is when one's civil rights are removed. People feel secure in their own environment; they know their rights and their obligations. When those rights are terminated, when the social, environmental, or even meteorological framework that give people a sense of security are altered – that person will feel like a stranger in his own land. *Avdus* means enslaved, a situation in which one's personal liberty is curtailed, and his individual possessions – those that underscore his identity – are removed. Like a de-personalized serf, his very individuality is removed, and he becomes his master's chattel. Finally, there is the abject state of *inuy*, which is physical discomfort and abuse.

In the precise manner foretold by Hashem to Avraham, the servitude in Egypt began. In a sequence eerily reminiscent of more modern German times, the Jewish population at first suffered from discrimination that curtailed their civil rights, then their personal human rights, and finally they suffered the pain, indignity, and the anguish of physical suffering.

In whatever manner one conducts himself, Divine judgment deals with him in a similar manner (Sotah 8b). Thus, the judgments and punishments inflicted upon the Egyptians followed the preset pattern. The ten plagues were divided into three groups, and each group contained three plagues; one of *geirus*, one of *avdus*, and the final one in each group, *inuy*.

By the plague of blood, the Egyptians were made to feel like strangers in their own land. When you go to the sink for a glass of water, you do not entertain the slightest doubt that water will come out of the tap. If red, turgid, slowly congealing blood would ooze from the open tap, you would feel decidedly uncomfortable and shocked. Imagine waking up one fine morning, sleepily reaching for the *negel vasser*, only to find a strange, sticky, slimy sensation as you pour the contents of the cup over your hand. You would jump out of bed in horror and disbelief. Imagine dipping your head to the tap in the bathroom to rinse out your mouth after brushing your teeth, and instead of cold refreshing water, you find your mouth filled with gooey, mucous-like, clotting blood. You would recoil in horrified shock. You would not believe that this could be happening. These things don't happen in Egypt! Water is water, not thick blood. You would feel threatened, not comprehending, and insecure. You would feel like a stranger in your own land.

Every person has a pride and sense of confidence about his possessions. They are a part of him, an extension of his individual personality. As you go about your house, you do not think twice about sitting on a chair, opening a cupboard, putting on your clothes, or – at the day's end – resting your weary head on the pillow. Your personal possessions allow you function, to live and be the person you wish to be. Along came the frogs. *They shall ascend and come into your palace and your bedroom and your bed, into your oven and into your kneading bowls...* (*Shemos* 7:28). Open your cupboard to take out a plate, out jumps a frog, sad to relate. Not just a single, "Oh my, that's so cute, a little sweet frog," but the cupboard was teeming with green slimy amphibians. It was not cute, it was disgusting. Suddenly, their possessions were not their own. In their beds, in their shoes, in the breakfast cereal, on the chair, under the pillow, in their hats, behind the door, under the mat – everywhere the ubiquitous green slimy, toady, croaking frogs. They lost their personal space, their treasured possessions. Just like the slaves.

Now, with the third plague in the series, the insecurity and the inconvenience became magnified and painful, as all the dust of the land turned into lice. Egypt is a dusty, sandy place. When the Torah says, *All the dust of the land became lice* (ibid. 8:13), we're talking about a lot of lice. Everywhere. There was no escape. All over their bodies, in their hair, endlessly they scratched and groaned in despair. The pain and agony that the Egyptians endured reflected that which they had inflicted on their Jewish slaves, measure for measure.

In the second set in the series of plagues, the pattern repeats itself. When a person lives in a particular location, one of the factors that enables him to feel secure in that place is the comfort of knowing how things work. People in Gateshead know that the traffic travels on the left, and feel assured when crossing the road that no vehicle is going to unexpectedly approach from the wrong direction. Jewish people in any location feel generally safe when interacting with the local populace because they feel familiar with the mindset of the locals, whereas a visitor might feel nervous in that same situation, because he does not have the same sense of familiarity. Similarly, in any given country, the residents feel comfortable with the animals of that location, knowing which are tame, and of which care must be taken. An English visitor to Israel might be alarmed by the appearance of a lizard, sitting immobile on the wall of a bathroom, but his shriek of alarm would be smiled at by his Israeli host, who, accustomed to such things, would assure his guest that the little lizards are harmless – you see them all the time. If you would see a crocodile in the bath, then you can worry! No one in any country is concerned if a cat licks itself confidently as he approaches, or if a busy cluster of pigeons peck at a dropped biscuit – you know that as soon as you approach, they will scatter. Confident, assured citizen, forward you stride. Imagine your shock if the cat – instead of gliding under a fence – confronts you, with an arched back, glaring at you with fierce hostility, hissing menacingly! You stomp your foot nervously, and the cat fiercely approaches you, baring its teeth! Imagine your horror if the pigeons, instead of hopping away nervously, took to the air and headed in your direction – toward your eyes! Consider your consternation if, when opening your front door in response to a ring of the bell, you are confronted with a gorilla, mouth agape, emitting ferocious shrieks. In horror-stricken panic, you would race to the kitchen – only to find a tiger lurking behind the door in a crouched position, tensing itself to leap – in your direction. In horrified desperation, you reach for the telephone to call Emergency Services, and discover, too late, that you have grasped the poisonous python wrapped around the phone. In your desperation to escape the marauding animals, you feel like a total stranger in your land. Never knowing which member of this unprecedented menagerie will be lurking around the next corner, you wish you could relocate to any country, anywhere, to be away from the land that suddenly has made you feel a stranger.

The animal epidemic that afflicted the Egyptians devastated their treasured possessions. In the lives of farming communities, wealth was measured by heads of cattle and flocks of sheep. The mysterious epidemic that befell the animals owned by Egyptians – while leaving every single Jewish-owned animal immune, deprived the Egyptians of their wealth. Livestock: horses, donkeys, camels, sheep – all fell to the silent killer that, at a stroke, impoverished the Egyptians. From one day to the next, they discovered how it felt to be a dispossessed slave.

Nothing could have been more personally agonizing than the unprecedented and spontaneous outbreak of boils. When a person suffers from a pain in his foot, at least he has another foot on which to stand. A painkiller can ameliorate the throbbing pain of a toothache. But no one wishes to imagine the agony of a body covered with bulbous, bulging, bursting blisters and boils; impossible to sit, painful to stand, no comfortable position for lying in bed. What's more, there was no one to attend to the running sores, since everyone was experiencing the same agony – constant unadulterated stress and torment – exactly like the distress and torment that their cruel whips and relentless beatings had caused their Jewish slaves.

The third set of plagues faithfully followed the same pattern. Anyone living in a country grows accustomed to the climate in that location. Residents in Toronto are unfazed by plummeting temperatures and heavy snowfalls in the long winter months. *Yidden* fortunate enough to live in our Holy Land do not generally complain about the hot summer months, where the very ground seems to shimmer in the reflected heat of the fierce sun. Grey skies and drizzling rain are as uniquely British as the Changing of the Guards. You know your country, and you know your weather. The very last thing an Egyptian expects as he looks at the clear blue sky is a hail storm. Rashi (*Shemos* 7:17) tells us that there was no rain in Egypt. The Nile River provided their water, and the seasonal flooding of the river irrigated the surrounding land. Suddenly, as if from nowhere, the country was hammered by a hail storm of ferocious intensity – thunder, lightning, and hail stones with fiery centers – unrelenting and unprecedented. They don't sell umbrellas in Egypt. All of a sudden, the Egyptians did not recognize their country. Hail storms like this didn't happen anywhere – let alone in the parched, sun-soaked, arid desert climate of Egypt. As an Egyptian waded through the water, one hand covering his head in desperate attempt to protect himself from missile-like hail stones, the other hand clapped against his ear to muffle the crashing noise, he felt disorientated and frightened – a stranger in his own land.

Whatever pitiful possessions the Egyptians still had after the devastating plagues of animal pestilence and hail were eagerly consumed by the voracious locusts. Like a moving cloud, the swarm of locust descended, and with insatiable hunger, they devoured every blade of grass, every fruit on every tree; every stalk of wheat and spelt – whatever had survived the hail – was eaten. The Egyptians were left with nothing. Bare fields, trees with skeletal branches, gardens with nothing growing, vacant echoing cupboards – like slaves with nothing to eat – that is exactly how they felt, and what indeed they were.

What affliction could be more poignant than total absence of light? To stumble around for three days in all-enveloping darkness with the terrible fear of the unknown; why was this happening? Would they ever regain their sight? How could they live in black sightlessness? This was an affliction beyond a nightmare – which was then compounded by an inexplicable inability to move. For three days they were frozen in statuesque immobility, as if turned into stone. Imagine the terror in their minds as they thought that they would be doomed to this sightless petrified state forever! Imagine their discomfort, their thirst and hunger, their fear. This was the ultimate physical affliction – a fitting climax to the decades-long physical abuse of their Jewish slaves. Fitting, exact, and precise. Measure for measure, exactly as foretold.

EIGHTEEN
The Most Reluctant Leader

Of all the qualities required to become President of the United States, there is no doubt that the chief of all requirements is ambition. In the political system most favored by Western civilization, the system of democracy, people vote for representatives to govern the state on their behalf. A person wishing to be voted for by a specific constituency, whether a state or a whole country, must want his name to appear on the voting list. His name does not appear by accident, or against his will. And he has to want his name to appear very much.

In the long process of wishing to be chosen for the most coveted position, the candidate has to demonstrate his worth to those choosing him. He has to be industrious – showing commitment to his political party; tireless – willing to work long hours in the furtherance of his aim; zealous – demonstrating great enthusiasm for the ideals that his political party espouses; and above all, he must possess the desire, the powerful desire, to advance his position. To be selected for a coveted place on the electoral ballot, the would-be candidate has to cultivate friendships with the great and powerful groups who wield influence, convincing them of his sterling qualities, ingratiating himself to them, saying the right things and cultivating the right image to assure them that he is the best choice for the job.

In the American system of government, an ambitious aspirant for the presidency has to gain the nomination of one of the two main political parties. Attaining that position requires all the persuading and smooth-talking that is possible. He has to convince his supporters that he offers the best chance for the victory of his party. He has to state very clearly why his qualities are superior to his fellow contenders. Modesty and bashfulness are put into cold-storage as he confidently and forcefully describes his unique attributes.

Once the treasured nomination has been attained, the presidential nominee, driven by an insatiable desire to occupy the White House, has a tough job. He has to select a talented group of people, well versed in the techniques of psychology, advertising, presentation, speech-writing, and image-creating, to plan his election campaign. Amongst his selected team will be investigative journalists whose task will be to discover negative statements, activities, and personal foibles of his opponent. The whole campaign costs a lot of money. In the 2012 presidential contest, Barack Obama raised 690 million dollars. Wanting to become US President requires not only ambition, but also great wealth – or at least the ability to raise enormous sums.

The presidential race has no place for grace or kind sentiments concerning one's rival. Winston Churchill's famous dismissal of a political opponent – "The noble gentleman is very modest, but there again, he has much to be modest about" – would seem a great compliment compared to the sometimes-savage verbal attacks thrown by one presidential candidate against the other.

Most of the advertising in the 2012 presidential campaign was decidedly negative, pointing out the faults of the opponent rather than the positive aspects of their own ideology. It was found that 80 percent of the advertisement produced by Obama and 84 percent of those issued by his opponent Romney were negative. Sorry, *shemiras halashon*, I've an election to win!

Gaining insight into the political process is not only interesting from the perspective of an understanding of the human condition, it is also invaluable in enabling us to contrast it with the choice of Moshe Rabbeinu as leader of the Jewish People in the period of the Exodus. Never in Jewish history was a qualified leader as crucial as it was now, during the time that Hashem would bring His people from Egypt, cross the Red Sea, communicate with them at Mount Sinai, lead them on a forty-year odyssey through the desert, and bring them to their Promised Land. This was the time that Hashem would demonstrate convincingly and unequivocally that He alone achieved that which was humanly impossible to achieve – the release of the Jews from their Egyptian prison with the accompaniment of ten plagues. It was absolutely imperative that the chosen leader would be someone who no one could ever think had his own political ambitions. The man selected to lead his people would obviously require prodigious spiritual qualities – he would be the greatest of all the prophets – but in terms of human ambition or a drive to lead, it was vital that those characteristics should be absent. The slightest possibility that the leader had a personal interest or agenda in becoming leader would proportionally diminish the uniqueness of Hashem's direct involvement.

Bearing all this in mind, we shall see that Moshe Rabbeinu was the perfect choice. The Torah records that when Hashem appeared to Moshe and informed him of his appointment to lead the Jewish People, Moshe strenuously resisted. *"Who am I that I should go to Pharaoh and that I should take the Children of Israel out of Egypt?"* (*Shemos* 3:11). Moshe considered himself entirely unqualified for this historic task – and looking at it from Moshe's perspective, we can well understand why. Moshe had been away from Egypt for forty years. The people down in Egypt did not know him, and those who had known him must have long forgotten about him.

"Didn't Aharon once have a younger brother?"

"Well, yes. Remember that incident with the Egyptian who attacked the Jew?"

"Oh yes! He had to run away. I wonder what happened to him? Haven't heard about him for years!"

Additionally, Moshe suffered from a speech impediment. *"Please, my Lord, I am not a man of words...for I am heavy of mouth and heavy of speech"* (ibid. 4:10). It is axiomatic that a person will not dream of performing a task for which he knows he is absolutely unqualified. A person who is scared of heights and feels queasy when standing on a chair to change a light bulb will not dream of climbing Mount Everest. A fledgling *yeshivah bachur*, who just about knows which way to hold his Gemara, will not realistically dream of giving the opening *shiur* to the whole yeshivah – to which all the town's *roshei yeshivah* have been invited. Particularly if the *shiur* has to be given in Yiddish, and this sweet new *bachur's* command of Yiddish consists of three words: *Ich veiss nisht*. A man with a speech impediment, whether a stammer or a stutter, someone to whom listening to requires patience, will not dream of standing in front of the world's mightiest – and cruelest – tyrant, pleading the cause of his own people. People do not entertain dreams when those dreams are nightmares.

And, above all, Moshe was a younger brother. All younger brothers will recognize the "younger brother syndrome." Whereas oldest brothers (or sisters) occupy a position of privilege and responsibility within the family, often occupying the role of junior parent, and youngest brothers (or sisters) are treated with special affection, younger brothers are hardly looked at. They follow their older sibling's example, wear the clothes that are passed down to them, no one usually asks their opinions, they sit quietly in the corner sucking their thumb, and go through childhood largely unnoticed. They do not aspire to leadership roles – that's big brother's prerogative, they are not big decision makers within the family – their opinion is rarely asked, and so they live their lives in peaceful serenity and semi-obscurity. They live in the shadow of those more senior, and do not entertain dreams of altering their role. Moshe had an older brother, called Aharon. Aharon lived in Egypt, was known and revered by his fellow Jews, spoke without impediment, and would always have expected, in the natural order of things, to assume a position of leadership. In addition to Moshe's natural modesty and self-effacement (*Now the man Moshe was exceedingly humble, more* than any person on the face of the earth! [*Bamidbar* 12:3]), his family position as younger brother ensured that he would never entertain dreams and ambitions of becoming a leader of his people. That was Aharon's job. For seven days, Moshe resisted the Divine command to assume leadership – because he had an older brother. How would Aharon feel if his younger brother became a leader? *"Please, my Lord, send through whoever You will send"* (*Shemos* 4:13) – meaning Aharon.

This goes even further. I heard from my *rebbi*, Harav Mattisyahu Salomon *shlit"a*, that it is well known that the Torah is not a story book. Had it been so, there would have been ample space – several chapters perhaps – devoted to a detailed description of Moshe's early years. Instead, the Torah tells us one single fact, with an illustration of three small incidents. The fact: *It happened in those days that Moshe grew up and went out to his brethren and observed their burdens* (ibid. 2:11).

Rashi explains that Moshe demonstrated the quality of empathy, sensitivity to his brothers' plight, and was anxious to share their burden. This quality is illustrated by three incidents: coming to the assistance of a Jewish man suffering an attack by an Egyptian, intervening when he saw two Jewish men arguing with one about to be struck, and finally – after fleeing to Midyan – coming to the assistance of Yisro's daughters, saving them from the molesting locals.

This then was his great characteristic. A sensitivity to others. The ability to put himself in their position with total empathy. Now he is being told to go down to Egypt and assume the leadership of the Jewish People, leading them to freedom. But he has an elder brother! That older brother is bound to be upset! Which normal person would not be disappointed to see the choice position – one that he might well have assumed was his for the taking – going to his younger brother who could hardly speak? And Moshe was the most sensitive man when it came to others' feelings. That means that Moshe Rabbeinu had never once, in his entire eighty years, dreamt, or wanted, or wished – or thought that he was going to be the leader.

That was the absolute cast-iron guarantee that Moshe Rabbeinu's appointment as leader was totally and completely a Divine command – and the very furthest possible from the realization of a personal ambition.

If ever there was a man who was the absolute opposite of a career-politician, someone who never for one moment entertained ambitions of leadership, or considered that there was any possibility of being chosen for that role – it was Moshe. And it was for that very reason that Moshe was chosen; so that no one would ever have cause to suspect that Moshe was a self-appointed, grandeur-seeking, political-style leader. With all his unique qualities of greatness it had to be – and was – abundantly clear that the release of the Jewish people from their Egyptian prison was solely through Divine agency, and that Moshe was the absolutely reliable, humble, self-effacing *eved ne'eman*, most reluctant leader and trusted servant.

NINETEEN
The Truth

Readers of popular Jewish literature will know that the last forty years have seen a plethora of story books. Some are full-length novels; others are collections of inspiring stories. There are those that are unashamedly fictitious, but present Jewish themes and claim value by dealing with issues and challenges with which the reader can identify, and thus gain knowledge, strength, or insight. Some honestly state that the story they relate is based on true historical facts, so that the reader knows that while the details, and even the plot, are products of the author's fertile imagination, the possibility of the theme and location details are somehow linked to reality. There are stories where the source is given, although names have been changed to protect privacy, so that the hero Chaim Yankel could just as well be Norman Stewart. Perhaps the most tantalizing are those books that contain inspiring stories with heart-warming and thought-provoking content that enable the reader to soar in his imagination to heights of elation, idealism, and commitment; they allow the avid reader to walk in the footsteps of plausible Jewish heroes – and really have the power to change lives – but fail to mention in the glowing inside-covers a single most-important word. This is the word the reader is anxiously seeking. Truth. Are these stories true; can I allow myself to be genuinely inspired and alter my mindset, firm in the knowledge that the stories really happened, precisely as described? Or – and in the doubt lies the dread – the tales are amazing, breathtaking, and gripping, but like dream-stuff, figments of a rich, active imagination. The reader is reluctant to be inspired because of the strong possibility that it is all fictitious. Why give away your emotions and mind – for nothing? Tell me that the stories are true and I shall digest and enjoy the contents, emboldened and invigorated by the powerful message; but failure to mention that all-important word and keep the reader guessing, is to dilute much of the value. Just like a multi-colored photograph of a delicious meal will not satisfy a hungry man if the picture is in a cookbook, so an amazing story that denies you knowledge of veracity remains a single-dimensional flat apparition, inspiring no one. Enjoyable for sure, but mind-changing and life-altering? How do I know the stories are true?

The Jews are called "The People of the Book." The Book that has given us that illustrious title is the one that has consistently remained the world's best-selling publication, has influenced billions of inhabitants around the globe throughout the centuries, has been translated into every language from Welsh to Swahili, will be found in every hotel room and hospital locker – it is the Bible, otherwise known as *Tanach*, *The Old Testament*, or *The Five Books of Moses*. (The audacity and chutzpah of the other nations in taking their "holy" book, printing it together with the Torah, and giving it the name "*The Holy Scriptures*" is analogous of taking a bunch of cheap comics, *Superman Annual* and *The*

Best of Mickey Mouse, printing it together with the complete works of William Shakespeare, and calling it *"Great Works of British Literature."*) Our Torah – the Written Law – contains a sentence that guarantees its reliability and assures its worldwide and eternal readership of its veracity: *Distance yourself from a false word* (Shemos 23:7).

R' Bunim of P'schischa observed that regarding no other transgression does the Torah say that one should *distance* oneself. So much does G-d abhor falsehood that we are commanded to stay far – even from an appearance of a lie.

Every intelligent person will realize that writing a phrase in which the readership is enjoined to abhor falsehood is to issue a serious challenge. The readership of the Book containing the warning to "stay far away from falsehood" is challenged to investigate the Book thoroughly, to check it through and through, examine every fact, search every claim, probe every name and date, test every prediction, and explore every single detail. If you can discover a single falsehood in but one tiny detail, even the smallest inconsistency even in a seemingly unimportant point, then the Book will be invalidated. If you would compose a book containing imaginative stories, full of fiction and fancy, you would not claim, "These stories are entirely true." If you wished to gain fame and fortune by compiling information on zoology, botany, and biology, none of which had been investigated or verified, and then published your fascinating concoction, you would never use the precious term "true" in the book description. The folly and hollowness of your claim would be uncovered by the first reader.

The Truth

If the writer of a book writes, "Keep away – far away – from falsehood," he is announcing to the whole world – contemporary and future – that every single fact, detail, and nuance contained in the book is absolutely and one hundred percent true.

Suppose the claim of truth was printed on a book containing vague sentiments – "Seasons come and go, but friendships last forever," "No one cares how much you know until they know how much you care," "Early to bed, early to rise makes you healthy, wealthy, and wise" – sweet sayings and cute quotations which can never be quantified, investigated, proven, or negated. But the risk is low. The sayings are more or less correct, and like tepid water, will harm no one nor excite anyone. But the Torah deals with hard facts. It describes the history of the world from Creation until the passing of Moshe. In doing so, it gives precise details of the line of descent from the original Adam for some twenty-six generations. The Torah deals with historical events that affected the world – the Flood, the Dispersion – in great detail. In the case of the Flood, we know the date the rain began falling, the dimensions of the Ark, how high above the mountain peaks the water reached, when the rain stopped, when Noach stepped out of the Ark, and which people were fortunate enough to be his companions during his enforced voyage. The Torah contains detailed information on matters of biology, botany, zoology, horticulture, astronomy, psychology, and physics. The Torah gives precise and detailed predictions of the consequences of compliance with and non-compliance of its laws, consequences which affect not just individuals, whose fate and fortune might not be widely known, but whole nations, whose destiny can be accurately charted and examined. It is in this Book that the Writer has declared in clear letters of black on white, *Keep away from falsehood*. No one issues a challenge of that description about a book that contains the totality of knowledge in every subject without absolute confidence that the challenge cannot be repudiated.

It is well known that Martin Luther – no friend of the Jews – who broke away from the established Catholic Church in Germany in 1517 to begin the Reformation Movement, decried the refusal of the church authorities to translate the "Bible" into German. It had to remain written in the language which virtually no one understood – Latin. The obdurate refusal of the Catholics to allow the masses to understand their Scriptures was understandable. They did not want their followers to comprehend the Book – that might lead to some uncomfortable questions for which there might not be answers. Their Bible had to be remote, revered, and inaccessible. The priests would pretend to comprehend, and they, holy men that they were, would deliver the relevant messages to the great masses of simple and untutored folk. Much better that they should not understand it. Not exactly a ringing affirmation of truth.

Contrast this to our teachings, in which the primary mitzvah of every Jew is to study: *The study of the Torah is equivalent to them all* (*Shabbos* 127a). He studies at home, away from home, day and night, he dedicates years of his life – and sometimes an entire lifetime – to study. Wives voluntarily accept responsibilities of livelihood to allow their husbands to study extra years. Study halls are alive and buzzing during the day as well as at night while the world sleeps. The proudest moment of Jewish people is when their son arrives at the grand age of three years old, when the little lad is carried in pomp and ceremony to his teacher to begin studying the Torah. Not a day passes, not a meal is eaten, without Torah study. *For they* (words of Torah) *are our life and length of our days, and about them we will meditate day and night* (Ma'ariv Prayer).

The greatest minds and giants of intellect, together with everyday folk, all share a common ambition: to study the Torah. Other nations have sports, politics, entertainment, military conquests, and travel to occupy their minds and fill their days. The Jewish Nation, from young to old, on a working day and on vacation, day after day and every day, fill their time with a simple passion – studying the Torah, plumbing its depths, unraveling its intricacies, asking penetrating questions and analyzing the texts, a question, an answer, a challenge, a refutation, a proof, a contradiction, a solution, a discovery, a new insight, a spectacular discovery – this is our relationship with the Torah.

No text anywhere in the world, no body of learning, has been so closely scrutinized and analyzed as the Torah. Not for one year, but for 3,326 years, every single day, with no exception. Hashem knew the people to whom He was entrusting the Torah. He gave the command to study the Torah in its primacy,[1] and

---

1. *This Book of the Torah shall not depart from your mouth, rather you should contemplate it day and night...* (*Yehoshua* 1:8).

when He wrote, *Distance yourself from a false word*, He knew He had nothing to fear. In a world of uncertainty one thing is certain. Torah is the Truth.

TWENTY
The Whole Truth

It is the custom of many observant Jews to articulate the word "Shabbos" many times on Shabbos. Whether the custom has a source, or whether it is simply common practice, is uncertain, but careful observation of our friends around us will reveal just how widespread this custom is. As Shabbos approaches, Jews everywhere are gripped with a sense of mild panic. Whatever activity they are engaged in, they mutter, "*S'iz bald Shabbos*" ("It's nearly Shabbos") and speed up their activity. Fathers urge their children to prepare themselves for the great day by declaring repeatedly, "*Kinderlach, Shabbos!*" ("Children, Shabbos!") At the termination of evening prayers, and thereafter throughout the Holy Day – everyone wishes everyone else, "Good Shabbos," with the stress on the word Shabbos. The proliferation of this greeting is such that there are pious folk who wish each other "Good Shabbos" from some time on Thursday, causing a degree of consternation to the recipients of the greeting who wonder, upon hearing "Good Shabbos" at the end of a conversation on Thursday afternoon, whether they have woken up on the correct day. There is something magical about a steaming plate of cholent – that special Shabbos elixir – that causes the recipient, usually male, to smile beatifically and mutter happily, "Ah, Shabbos!" When, after an overdose of cholent, the gentleman retires to his bedroom and lays his drowsy head on the soft pillow, he will be heard to repeat, "Ah! Shabbos," several times at progressively softer levels as sweet sleep overtakes him.

Jewish people love their Shabbos and are inexorably bound to it for all eternity, and their repeated enunciation of "Shabbos" on that holy day is but an expression of that unbreakable bond.

In a similar way, but in a manner that can be accurately quantified, the Torah's preoccupation with truth is remarkable. The Hebrew word for truth is *emes* – אמת. The words of Tehillim 119:160, *Your very first utterance is truth...*, refer to the first three words of the Torah, בראשית ברא אלקים – the three end letters of which comprise אמת – truth. Looking at the second, third, and fourth word in the Torah will demonstrate exactly the same phenomenon: ברא אלקים את. Even more remarkably, the last three words in the Torah's account of Creation are ברא אלקים לעשות – the end letters of which formulate אמת. In other words, the Torah is transmitting a message loud and clear that its description of the Creation is encapsulated by אמת – Truth.

A fascinating fact that underscores the Torah's preoccupation with truth is that if you examine the first verse in *Bereishis*, you will find every single vowel sound. They are all there – except for one. The "*oo*" (as in "moon") sound is conspicuous by its absence. Where is it? When you discover that the name given to that particular sound is "*shooruk*" – שרק, all becomes clear. שרק are the three letters comprising שקר – untruth – the antithesis of *emes*. The Torah wishes to distance itself from falsehood to the extent of omitting a certain vowel sound from its initial *pasuk*.

The Whole Truth

Continuing the theme of truth, the concluding three words of the Torah are *before the eyes of all Israel*, referring to the many miracles and wonders that accompanied the ten plagues and the Exodus from Egypt. Everyone witnessed everything. In stark contrast, in many man-made religions, a charismatic character attempts to convince potential followers of a Divine visitation or some private revelation. Their willingness to believe his story will depend on the founder's power of persuasion and the follower's gullibility, whereas the Torah tells us that all the people witnessed everything firsthand. I can try to convince you what happened to me – you either believe me or you do not – but I cannot sell you a story that happened to you!

Dovid Hamelech encapsulates the feelings of the Jewish People regarding truth: *I have hated falsehood and abhorred it; Your Torah I love*. Hate and abhor are powerful words which adequately express the repugnance that the author feels for falsehood – whereas in absolute contrast stands the Torah, a shining citadel of truth. If the Torah peppers its opening paragraphs with *emes*, we should not be surprised if it encodes the antithesis of truth – *sheker* – in its description of Amalek's dastardly deeds. Sure enough, in the passage commanding us to remember Amalek, we read the phrase אשר קרך בדרך (*Devarim* 25:18), *that he happened upon you on the way*. The three bold letters form the word שקר, epitomizing the nature of the arch-enemy, arch-denier of G-d.

In the language of the Torah, *Lashon Hakodesh*, every letter equates to a number. The word אמת is comprised of three letters, א=1, מ=40, ת=400, so that the complete word has a numerical value of 441. Adding up those three digits gives the number 9 (4+4+1). The uniqueness of that number is its indestructibility. However you multiply 9, the digits will always add up to 9 (9x45=405; 9x361=3,249=18=9). The meaning is clear. Just like the addition of its digits formulates an indestructible number, so אמת itself is an indestructible entity that nothing can break.

It is surely no coincidence that the word אמת extends over the whole *aleph-beis*, representing the first, last, and the middle letter. (Keen students will wonder how, if the *aleph-beis* is comprised of twenty-two letters, you can have a middle letter. You cannot have a middle of an even number. However, when you include the final letters, you have twenty-seven, and *mem* sits in the middle with thirteen letters to either side.) Thus, *emes* encompasses everything contained therein.

א ב ג ד ה ו ז ח ט י כ ך ל מ ם נ ן ס ע פ ף צ ץ ק ר ש ת

An interesting perspective to the wide separation of the letters of *emes*, is that when you have two or three witnesses to a fact, each one secure in the knowledge that he is relating the truth, you can separate the witnesses, question them individually, and each one will confidently recount the same story. They do not require each other's company to corroborate their fellow witness's story – *Split us up, ask us whatever you'd like, we are telling the truth.* Whereas, if the three witnesses are indeed false, they need to huddle together, each one trying to support the other in order to bolster their account of events. Separating them will quickly reveal the glaring discrepancies in their false report. So, in contrast to א-מ-ת in which each letter happily agrees to be separate from its friend, שקר is comprised of three letters huddled together for mutual protection at the alphabet's end. *Don't separate us – we will not stand up to scrutiny.* There they stand, almost at the end. Almost, but not quite. For falsehood can never have the last word!

In a remarkable combination of letters, the Torah emphasizes the need to teach children truth. In *Parshas Re'eh* (11:19), we see the phrase ולמדתם אתם את בניכם – *You shall teach them to your children.* In the sequence of letters beginning with the letter ת in the first word, proceeding to the next two letters (מ-א), you find the word אמת. Then, skipping one letter and beginning with the next מ, again we have the word אמת (scrambled). This three-letter sequence of the word *emes* can be seen *five times* in the space of the underlined seven letters. There could not be a more powerful message relayed by the Author of the Torah. *V'Hashem Elokim emes* – "Hashem, G-d, is true" (*Yirmiyahu* 10:10).

TWENTY-ONE
And Nothing but the Truth

The story – true or not – is told of a challenge issued by church fathers to a Jewish community to debate religious issues. A representative from both "religions" would meet at a specified time and location, and the first one to admit ignorance to any given question would concede victory to his opponent. In days of religious intolerance and persecution, a defeat for the Jewish camp could only have severe repercussions.

As could be imagined, there was no rush to volunteer for the position of representative amongst the Jewish community. Who could guarantee success in this dangerous situation, and who would wish to take responsibility for the consequences of failure? Quite unexpectedly, a simple tailor stepped forward and volunteered his services. "I am happy to represent our *kehillah*," he said confidently. When asked how he could be so confident of defeating the church representative, given that his level of learning was basic in the extreme, he calmly dismissed their doubts and skepticism and told them not to worry.

The great day arrived, and in the Great Hall sat gathered all the church dignitaries, the panel of judges, the church representative of haughty bearing, the frightened members of the Jewish community, and the humble tailor, who stood straight and calm, with no visible trace of nervousness. With feigned graciousness, the church authorities declared that the Jews could pose the first question. With not a second's pause, the tailor said, "Could you, Priest, please tell me the correct translation of the words *eini yode'a mah milamdeinu*?"

"Not a problem," answered the priest smugly, "I don't know what it comes to teach us."

It was as if a bomb had exploded. Shock and disbelief gripped the crowd as the impact of the priest's words took effect. In agitated consternation, the judges hastily convened and in a quavering voice declared the tailor triumphant. The debate was over before it had begun.

Exiting the hall in relief and happiness, the Jewish spectators crowded around the tailor, who appeared bemused and unaffected by the euphoria surrounding him. "How did you think of that?" his friends asked. "Who gave you the brilliant idea to ask that question?"

His response was unexpected. "I really don't know what all the fuss is about. It's all very simple. Every week I learn the *parshah* with Rashi, and, not being very skilled with translating, I look at my *Ivri teitch* (Yiddish translation) to see what the *pasuk* says and how Rashi explains it. Well, as you know, in *Parshas Toldos* the *pasuk* tells us that Yitzchak sent away Yaakov, and he went toward Padan Aram to Lavan, the son of Besuel the Aramean, brother of Rivkah, *mother of Yaakov and Eisav* (*Bereishis* 28:5). I looked into Rashi and all he says is four words, *eini yode'a mah milamdeinu*. Now, I don't know what that means, so I looked in the *Ivri teitch* and there he says, *Ich veiss nisht vos dos kumt unz tzu lernen* – 'I don't know what it comes to teach us.' So I thought, I don't know what Rashi means and the wise *Ivri teitch* doesn't know what Rashi means, so for sure the *galach* won't know what it means!"

The humble tailor, everyone's hero, is revealing a great factor in the Torah's veracity. That Rashi – the paramount commentator of Torah, *Nevi'im*, and *Kesuvim*, and virtually all of *Shas* – is not embarrassed to admit that there is something in the Torah that he does not understand. To fully comprehend Rashi's greatness in this admission, we have to be aware that Rashi does not comment on every word. There are countless *pesukim* on which Rashi offers no commentary whatsoever. Rashi did not have to admit that he does not understand why the Torah writes words that seem superfluous. He could have happily kept silent and no one would have been the wiser. Why tell the whole world what you don't understand?

But therein lies the greatness. Rashi did not write down his commentary for financial gain, or to garner fame. He was not seeking popular acclaim or vanity. His mission was to clarify the Torah, explain difficult concepts, and allow the reader a clearer insight into the Torah. He had one objective. To help future generations understand the Torah. Therefore, if there was a phrase for which Rashi could not find an explanation, part of his remit in clarifying the Torah is to inform us that there was a phrase that defied his understanding.

From where did Rashi learn this great and unremitting commitment to truth? From the Torah itself. In *Parshas Shemini*, we read how, after the tragic events of the day of the inauguration of the Tabernacle, in which the two elder sons of Aharon lost their lives bringing unwarranted incense, Moshe was annoyed that the sin-offering of Rosh Chodesh had not been eaten, but instead burned. Aharon took responsibility, explaining that there was a difference between a sacrifice relevant to that day, and a sacrifice which would be brought in the future, every Rosh Chodesh. *"If I had eaten the sin offering today* (in a state of mourning) *would it have been right in G-d's eyes?"* (*Vayikra* 10:19). When Moshe heard, he approved. The Gemara in *Zevachim* (101a) explains that Moshe conceded that Aharon was correct, and he was not tempted to deny having erred. Rather, he stated openly, "I heard this distinction, but I forgot it." The greatest authority in the Jewish Nation was not ashamed to admit that he had forgotten a detail of the law. Keen observers of politicians will have noticed that those men of ambition do not admit to mistakes, or take blame. When the agenda is pride, power, or vanity, an admission of error is a sign of weakness and failure, to be avoided at all costs. But when the agenda is truth, an admission of forgetfulness is more valuable than inflating one's reputation. Encapsulating the truthfulness that epitomizes Torah, the Gemara in *Brachos* 4 says, *Teach your tongue to say "I don't know."*

Rabbi Dr. Abraham Twerski, in his book *Living Each Week*, makes the point eloquently. In *Parshas Vayikra* (4:22), the Torah introduces the law of sin-offerings for the king with the words, *asher nasi yecheta* – "if the leader commits a sin." Rashi cites the Talmud which interprets *asher* as derived from *ashrei*, meaning "fortunate," and the verse thus reads, *Fortunate is the generation whose leader is willing to admit having sinned.*

Being a leader requires walking a fine line. On the one hand, the authority of the position must be maintained lest anarchy prevail, and on the other, a leader must be great enough to admit having been in error. Truth is central to the Torah, and is one of the foundations of the universe (*Pirkei Avos* 1:18). Adherence to the truth will not jeopardize one's authority.

Our greatest leader, Moshe, exemplified these qualities of leadership. To quell a rebellion against the authority of his leadership (*Bamidbar* 16:25), he made it absolutely clear that his position was of Divine origin (ibid. 16:29). Yet, when there was a question of law that he misinterpreted, Moshe did not hesitate to say that he was in error (*Vayikra* 10:20; Rashi).

Rav Chaim Shmulevitz *zt"l* cites the latter incident to emphasize the primacy of truth; that one may never fear that truth may result in harm. Moshe was the spokesman who conveyed the Divine word to Israel. Having heard Hashem speak to Moshe,[1] the Jewish People relied on Moshe's accuracy and reliability. When Moshe was confronted with the realization that he was incorrect in the understanding of a particular law, he could easily have rationalized that admitting his error would place the entire Torah in jeopardy. If Moshe was fallible, and if he was wrong in this particular instance, how could there be any assurance that he was not similarly mistaken in other laws?

---

1. *Behold I come to you in the thickness of the cloud so that the people will hear as I speak to you, and they will believe in you forever* (*Shemos* 19:9).

No one could have contradicted Moshe had he refused to yield and maintained the correctness of his position. He could have rationalized that admitting his error would place the authority of the Torah as being the Divine will in the greatest of dangers. How simple it would have been for him to say, "No, this is what G-d said." But Moshe knew that the truth would never endanger Torah. It is only falsehood that is a threat.

In the Talmud there are many instances when Jewish leaders vigorously defended the authority of their position, but had no difficulty admitting when they were in error. The Talmud therefore commends the leader who can admit to being wrong, and considers his generation to be fortunate.

TWENTY-TWO

No Protektzia

Imagine. Dwight D. Eisenhower was assigned to prepare for the Allied invasion of Europe in 1941. Two years later, he was appointed Supreme Commander of the Allied Expeditionary Forces for the invasion of France. Less than six months after that, on June 6, 1944, he sent one million men in some four thousand ships across the English Channel to Normandy in the largest amphibious landing in history. It was the turning point of World War II, and the beginning of the defeat of the hated Germans.

Imagine that on June 5, Eisenhower was being driven down to Dover to give the order for the invasion to commence. Pausing for a break, the driver, unfamiliar with English parking restrictions, parked the jeep on double yellow lines. Like a spider waiting for its prey, a highly conscientious police officer stepped in front of the jeep, licked his pencil, and began writing his parking ticket. Meanwhile, the army captain returned from his break and observed the scene. Restraining his anger with difficulty, he asked the officious official if he knew whose jeep this was. "I don't care whose jeep this is. He's parked on double yellow lines, and this jeep is not moving until the fine has been paid." The driver, in his sweetest but most menacing voice, asked the hapless cop if he was aware that a war was being fought, and that the passenger was no less than the illustrious Eisenhower, Supreme Commander of one million men, about to give the command to free enemy-occupied Europe, and if the pencil-touting minor policeman would not remove himself from his vulnerable position in front of the jeep, he might find himself in a very disadvantaged position underneath the jeep.

In the tapestry of truth that formulates the Torah, one of the central threads is the complete lack of favoritism shown to any of its heroes. Chief amongst them is Moshe our Teacher. If anyone should have deserved preferential treatment in return for a long career of dedication, devotion, and self-sacrifice, it should have been Moshe. Yet we see just the opposite. Time and again we read how Moshe Rabbeinu was treated with even-handed impartiality, in a manner unequaled in the world of privileged leadership.

After having been appointed the supreme leader of the Jewish People and receiving the blessing of his father-in-law, Moshe was on his way down to Egypt to begin the sequence of greatest events in history – the miraculous release of the enslaved Jewish Nation from Egypt, leading to the Revelation of G-d to His people at Mount Sinai. It was arguably the greatest mission in the history of mankind. Along the journey, G-d confronted Moshe *and wanted to kill him* (*Shemos* 4:24). The Gemara (*Nedarim* 31b) explains that when Moshe delayed the circumcision of his second son Eliezer, an angel immediately appeared to punish him for this lapse. It was only the expeditious intervention of Moshe's wife Tzipporah in circumcising her infant son that remedied the situation. Where was the immunity for leaders? Where was the exemption for people of high position? Where was the *protektzia*? There is none – *For Hashem, your G-d, He is the G-d of the powers and the Lord of the lords; the great, mighty, and awesome G-d Who does not show favor and Who does not accept a bribe* (*Devarim* 10:17).

It is human nature for a father to wish his son to succeed him and continue the family tradition. The Torah does not hide the fact that Moshe was desirous of one of his sons inheriting his position of leadership. When the daughters of Tzelafchad requested a possession of inheritance in the land of Israel in the absence of sons, their request was granted by Divine decree, and at that point the laws of priorities in inheritance were given. Immediately following, the Torah records Moshe's request that Hashem should appoint a leader, who would eventually take over the reins of leadership *and let the assembly of Hashem not be like sheep that have no shepherd* (*Bamidbar* 27:17). Rashi explains that the timing of the request was not coincidental. Now that Moshe had heard that Hashem had commanded him to transfer the inheritance of Tzelafchad to his daughters, Moshe thought that the time was appropriate to request his own needs, that his sons should inherit his position. Nothing would be more natural, and in any conventional dynasty, Moshe's request would have translated into reality. Indeed, in any comparable situation, no request would have been necessary. When you are in charge, you can do whatever you want.

This was no conventional situation. Moshe was not in charge. Moshe was Hashem's trusted servant. And his request was rejected. *Hashem said to Moshe, "Take to yourself Yehoshua son of Nun, a man in whom there is spirit, and lean your hands on him…* (ibid. 27:18). Moshe's two sons occupied no public position, and inherited no portion of their illustrious father's prominence. In the Torah of truth, there is no *protektzia*.

Imagine that you are planning a wedding. High on your list of priorities is assuring that your guests are comfortable at the various stages of the celebration. The more prominent your guests, the more care and thought you invest. At the *chuppah*, "reserved" notices inform the eager crowds that the seats directly facing the canopy are set aside for prominent personalities and members of the family. Similarly, at the dinner, the family heads and celebrants will confidently expect to be seated at the head table, or at the very least, in nodding distance of the exalted table. Close family would not be thrilled to be seated at the peripheries, near the washing area or close to the exit, where the constantly opening door allows the drafty air to cool their fast-diminishing enthusiasm. The closer the guest, the more concerned you feel for their comfort and well-being.

Imagine that you are Moshe, leading the Children of Israel ever closer to the Promised Land. Thought has been given to apportioning the land to the various tribes. Naturally, you want everyone to be happy, but you know that practically, not everyone will be able to occupy the choicest, most fertile areas of the land. As a leader, you like to treat everyone as a member of your family, but family is still family. And when your family is the Tribe of Levi, naturally you would wish to ensure that they, above everyone, should be satisfied and comfortable in their new, permanent abode. Capital city of Jerusalem? Well, naturally the Tribe of Levi should incorporate Jerusalem into their ancestral territory. Stands to reason. Where else should *kohanim* and *levi'im*, attendants of the Holy Temple, reside? Everyone would understand, and the Tribe of Levi might expect nothing less. In any other nation, in any similar situation, it would be so.

But this was no ordinary nation. *There shall not be for the kohanim, the levi'im – the entire Tribe of Levi – a portion and an inheritance with Israel; the fire-offerings of Hashem and His inheritance shall they eat. He shall not have an inheritance among his brethren; Hashem is his inheritance…* (Devarim 18:1-2).

There you are – the *chassan's* grandfather – you come to the wedding hall, confidently glancing through the place cards, until you are informed that there is no place for you at any table; but if you ask the guests comfortably seated at their designated places nicely, then they may give you a share of their main course! Surprised might be a mild reaction.

Having no provision of ancestral territory in effect deprived the *levi'im* of their source of livelihood. True, they were entitled to special agricultural gifts from their fellow Jews, but in essence, they would forever be dependent on the generosity of the other tribes for their sustenance. Scattered throughout the land in forty-eight designated cities, they would lack the security and ambiance of living together in territorial cohesion and unity. Moshe himself would never have consigned his own family to peripheral poverty, lacking the territorial facilities that were everyone else's rightful inheritance. But this was not Moshe himself. It was Hashem. *Hashem said to Aharon, "In their Land you shall have no heritage, and a share shall you not have among them; I am your share and your heritage among the children of Israel"* (*Bamidbar* 18:20). For the special Tribe of Levi – no *protektzia*.

And then, the greatest example of all. Moshe Rabbeinu wanted more than anything else to be permitted to enter the beautiful land that had been promised to his people. At any level, everyone can understand and sympathize with his request. From a spiritual, historic, and human perspective, Moshe yearned to complete the task for which he had been chosen. He yearned and he prayed. Not once, but 515 separate prayers to be permitted to enter. Had Moshe been a regular self-appointed leader, he would not have needed to ask anyone. You are in charge – go! But Moshe was not in charge. He was the trusted servant of Hashem, and was subservient to His wishes. For whatever good reason, permission was not granted, and Moshe ultimately accepted the edict and asked no more. The veracity of the Torah is accentuated and emblazoned when we read how our greatest leader had to subjugate his personal wishes to the will of the Creator. No favoritism, no special influence, no *protektzia*. Just truth.

TWENTY-THREE

The Greatest Event in History

You hear it before you see it; and when you see it you cannot believe it. As you approach the magnificent Niagara Falls, situated on the border of Canada and the United States, northwest of Buffalo and southwest of Toronto, the roar of thunder increases, obliterating all other sounds. Louder and louder, like the band at a *chasunah* that relentlessly turns the knob of the amplifier from loud to unbearable to deafening, the roar of water increases in volume, until in all its majesty, the magnificent Falls fill your field of vision, presenting you with a spectacle that is at once thrilling and awe-inspiring. On its way from Lake Erie to Lake Ontario, the Falls cascade over a drop that is 190 feet high and 1,050 feet wide in a roaring torrent that pours 3,160 tons of water over the edge every second. Viewed from above, the Falls appear like an ocean emptying away, with immense power and beauty, yet the flow never ceases. Twenty million people flock to witness the spectacle each year, and twenty million people each year assure their friends and families that it is a sight and experience that they will never forget; and rightly so. The force and majesty of the experience sears itself into their memory in an imprint that is indelible. Once seen, never forgotten.

The Greatest Event in History

Imagine an event in history, witnessed by millions of people simultaneously, whose thrill, power, and heart-stopping fear would make the Niagara Falls fade into insignificance. *Only take heed and watch yourself very carefully, so that you do not forget the things that your eyes saw. Do not let* (this memory) *leave your hearts, all the days of your lives. Teach your children and children's children about the day you stood before G-d your Lord at Chorev. It was then that G-d said to me, "Congregate the people for Me, and I will let them hear My words. This will teach them to be in awe of Me as long as they live on earth, and they will also teach their children"* (Devarim 4:9-10).

The Revelation of Hashem at Har Sinai was the epitome of powerful, both as an experience and in the facts it established. It makes absolute sense that the Creator Who created the world for a purpose would wish to make Himself known to the world, and specifically to the nation chosen to be His ambassadors and representatives to the world. It is part of the kindness of that revelation that it should be so powerful, so mind-filling and unequivocal, that never ever could there be a doubt in the collective memory of the people who experienced the event as to its veracity.

Indeed, we are told that the witnesses of the event; men, women, and children, were absolutely awestruck. *All the people saw the sounds, the flames, the blast of the ram's horn, and the mountain smoking. The people trembled when they saw it, keeping their distance. They said to Moshe, "You speak to us and we will listen, but do not let G-d speak to us anymore, for we will die if He does"* (Shemos 20:15-16). The sights, the sounds, the fire, the smoke, the mountain trembling, the blasts of the shofar increasing in volume and emanating from the terrifying backdrop, the sound of G-d...was an experience that would never be forgotten, ever.

There are many aspects of the Revelation that make it an event unique in history. Firstly, it was told to Moshe in advance. In the very first recorded speech of G-d to Moshe, he was told, *Proof that I have sent you will come when you get the people out of Egypt. All of you will then become G-d's servants on this mountain* (*Shemos* 3:12). Moshe – a passive emissary, the most reluctant leader ever born – was told at the very outset of his mission that the world's greatest event would take place on the very mountain on which communication began.

As the Jewish Nation, newly emerged from their Egyptian prison, camped around the mountain, they were given very specific instructions that would prepare them for the greatest event in history. G-d said to Moshe, *"Go to the people and sanctify them today and tomorrow. Let them immerse their clothing. They will then be ready for the third day, for on the third day, G-d will descend on Mount Sinai in the sight of all the people"* (*Shemos* 19:10-11). This Revelation, to the whole nation, at a pre-designated location, was no haphazard event, but pre-planned and pre-announced in the greatest detail to the people who would participate, with no active participation of Moshe, other than to be the conductor and leader of the people who would witness the unprecedented, most amazing single event ever experienced.

Hashem wanted the freshly formed Jewish Nation to be absolutely certain that His communication with them was totally devoid of any human involvement, and so, He commanded that immediately after the Revelation, when they hear the sound of the shofar emitting a long blast, they will then be allowed to climb the mountain (*Shemos* 19:13). This immediate access would permit them – even encourage them – to investigate and search for any device, any machinery, wires, amplifiers, or microphones, anything that could have artificially produced their experience.

This generation – every single member of the nation numbering millions – was chosen for the purpose of serving as eye-witnesses that would testify to all the generations that followed. And that is why, as Harav Avigdor Miller *zt"l* explains, the *pesukim* constantly reiterate that they saw.[1] For what can be more vital in an eye-witness account than the fact that they actually saw it all? Nothing; and that is why the Torah, in fact, concludes with the words, *Of all the Signs and Wonders that G-d sent him to do in the land of Egypt…and in all the mighty Hand and in all the great fear that Moshe wrought before the eyes of all Israel* (*Devarim* 34:12).

So we – unlike any other religion – had an entire generation of eye-witnesses. And we are the direct descendants of that generation; hence, the reliability of the transmission is absolute, and not a day goes by that we do not remind and recount to ourselves the event and its magnitude. We know that the Torah is the most reliable and accurate historical record ever written. We

---

1. *And all the people saw the sounds and the flames* (*Shemos* 20:15); *You have seen that from the Heavens I spoke with you* (ibid. 20:22); *And Israel saw the great Hand that G-d had done against Egypt* (ibid. 14:31); *And the Sons of Israel saw and they said to each other, "It is manna"* (ibid. 16:15).

know that if one letter is added or omitted from a *sefer Torah*, the whole *sefer Torah* is disqualified and may not be used. We know that every new *sefer Torah* that is written (an exercise that takes approximately a year and costs tens of thousands of dollars) is checked and re-checked to ensure its accuracy. We know that the Torah has a self-imposed safety mechanism that guarantees that nothing may be added or removed from the Torah – *You shall not add to the word that I command you, nor shall you subtract from it, to observe the commandments of Hashem your G-d, that I command you* (ibid. 4:2).

When the Torah is raised for everyone to see after reading from it, everyone exclaims, "*This is the Torah that Moshe placed before the Children of Israel*" (ibid. 4:44). It is in this Torah that the detailed events of the Revelation are recorded, and that record was given to the active participants. It was a record of that which they had personally experienced.

The Torah asks us to inquire whether anyone else makes a claim of a similar revelation. *You might inquire about times long past, going back to the time that G-d created man on earth, exploring one end of the heavens to the other; see if anything as great as this has ever happened, or if the like has ever been heard. Has any nation ever heard G-d speaking out of fire, as you have, and still survived? Has G-d ever done miracles, bringing one nation out of another nation with such miracles, signs, wonders, war, a mighty Hand and an outstretched Arm and terrifying phenomena, as G-d did for you in Egypt before your very eyes? You are the ones who have been shown, so that you will know that G-d is the Supreme Being, and there is none besides Him* (ibid. 4:32-35).

The Greatest Event in History

Every man-made religion would love to have this claim. Every nation would just be thrilled to refer back to a grand historic event where G-d gathered all their adherents and revealed Himself to them, informing them that they are His special people. What could be better?! The fact that not a single nation or religion has this claim is not through lack of wanting. If no one has this claim it is simply because it is impossible to fabricate an event of such magnitude, involving millions of people, and superimpose it on the fabric of history. If it could have been done, it would have been done countless times.

We know of the authenticity of the Revelation from the unbroken transmission that we have in the Torah, and the reliability and moral caliber of the transmitters. People looking for external verification will find it in the absence of any similar claim by the nations of the world – anytime, anyplace.

In terms of logic, historical accuracy, faultless and seamless transmission, mind-blowing experience, the Revelation of Hashem to His Chosen People can claim to be the one, single most-important event in history, unique and unprecedented. And it happened to our people!

You are the ones who have been shown, so that you will know that G-d is the Supreme Being and there is none besides Him (ibid. 4:35).

TWENTY-FOUR
Mitzvos That Testify

If you wish to gauge the measure of a nation, it would be worthwhile to study their laws. Countries that operate according to the system of democracy, in which the population choose their representatives to formulate their laws, will produce legislation that mirrors the mood and standards of the people. Freedom of speech, artistic expression, and freedom of access to all forms of information sits well with the liberal, mainly secular society, and so their desire for freedom is reflected in their laws. You may do what you wish so long as other members of society are not disturbed.

Dictators impose a rule of law that serves to promote and protect their power. Caring little for the feelings or benefits of the citizens, the megalomaniacal rulers seek only to perpetuate their grip on the levers of power. Like medieval serfs serving the insatiable appetite of the heartless barons, inhabitants of countries run by dictators suffer the oppressive regime, with physical escape from their countrywide prison their only hope.

Since the Torah is the repository of G-d's laws and the expression of G-d's will, careful scrutiny of some of those laws will demonstrate their unique qualities. Inasmuch as the Jewish Nation is uniquely privileged to be the representatives of G-d in the world, so do their laws give testimony to their Divine origin.

Members of the farming fraternity will know that overuse of land will deplete the nutrients that healthy plants require. Land, like humans, needs periodic rest to replenish energy levels. Problem is, while the land is enjoying its rest, nothing is growing. Nothing growing means nothing to eat. The solution is simple. Just like the owner of a large department store will organize his staff to take vacation at different times, allowing the store to remain open, so the farmer will divide his land into sections, or fields, permitting him to leave one area fallow each year, while working the others. Rotation is the key to success.

Having learned an essential lesson in basic farming economics, let us have a look at a law that was mentioned previously, which turns all conventional agricultural wisdom on its head. *Hashem spoke to Moshe on Mount Sinai, saying. Speak to the Children of Israel and say to them, "When you come into the land that I give you, the land should observe a Shabbos rest for Hashem. For six years you may sow your field…prune your vineyard…gather in its crops. But the seventh year shall be a complete rest for the land, a Shabbos for Hashem; your field you shall not sow, your vineyard you shall not prune…it shall be a year of rest for the land"* (*Vayikra* 25:1-5). The Torah is mandating a total shutdown of agricultural activity for a complete year. Nothing sown, nothing grown – just a year-long Shabbos. The emphasis on "a Shabbos for Hashem" is a categoric proclamation that this law of *shemittah* has little to do with agricultural benefits.

The Torah predicts that the recipients of this law might wonder how exactly they are to survive. Nothing sown; nothing grown –

nothing to eat! *If you will say, "What will we eat in the seventh year? Behold! We will not sow and not gather in our crops!"* It's a fair question and Hashem answers with a firm promise, *I will ordain My blessing for you in the sixth year and it will yield a crop sufficient for the three-year period* (ibid. 25:20-21). The powerful point here is to ponder whether any human being would, or could, legislate a law of this nature. Why would any person place his entire nation in the greatest jeopardy, endanger their survival with a year-long ban on any agricultural activity, and then issue a promise that he has absolutely no means of fulfilling? None of us has the ability to control the weather tomorrow, or to promise a bumper crop at any time. And as if to accentuate the problem, by the sixth year the land will be depleted of its vital nutrients, and if anything, the yield should be the lowest in the seven-year cycle. And lo and behold – the Torah promises a triple crop!

In case you thought this was insufficient, the Torah proceeds to give consequences to the observance of the *shemittah* year. Conscientious adherence to its laws will result in security and prosperity. *You shall perform My decrees, and observe My ordinances and perform them, then you shall dwell securely on the Land. The Land will give its fruit, and you will eat your fill; you will dwell securely upon it* (ibid. 25:18-19). Failure to observe its ordinances will have the reverse effect; desolation and the ruination of the land, and exile for its inhabitants.[1]

---

1. *Then the land will be appeased for its Sabbaticals during all the years of its desolation, while you are in the land of your enemies; for the land will rest and it will appease for its Sabbaticals. All the years of its desolation it will rest, whatever it did not rest during your Sabbaticals when you dwelled on it* (Vayikra 26:34-35).

All the laws of *shemittah* were given to the Jewish People before they even set foot into the Land of Israel. While still in the wilderness, they were given clear laws defining their responsibilities when, not if, they would settle in the land, and the clear and dire predictions of the consequences of their non-compliance with these laws. There is no logic that dictates that keeping religious laws results in prosperity, peace, and tranquility – and that famine, illness, and eventual exile flow from non-observance of these laws. No human king, prime minister, or president could make such a prediction. Only Hashem, Who enacts these laws, guarantees the safe arrival of the Jewish People to their Promised Land, and makes their continued successful sojourn in the land contingent on those laws, and has the ability to fulfill the detailed predictions, written for all to see. The law of *shemittah* is a testament to the Divine Author of the Torah.

Another law which cries "impossible" is the enactment – written in clear, unequivocal language – that commands the specially designated officer to send certain categories of soldiers back home from the battlefield.

The officers shall then speak to the people and say, "Is there any man among you who has built a new house and has not begun to live in it? Let him go home, so that he will not die in war and have another man live in it.

"Is there any man among you who has planted a vineyard and has not redeemed its first crop? (on its fourth year after planting) *Let him go home so that he not die in war and have another man redeem its crop.*

"Is there any man among you who has betrothed a woman and not married her? Let him go home, so that he not die in war and have another man marry her."

The officers shall then continue speaking to the people and say, "Is there any man among you who is afraid or fainthearted?[2] Let him go home rather than have his cowardliness demoralize his brethren."

Now everyone understands that war is a scary time. Particularly where the style of warfare was close combat, man against man with the clash of swords, the lunge of spears, and the incessant shower of deadly arrows flying through the air. No one knew which second would be his last. Courage does not mean to be devoid of fear – to the contrary – fear is a natural instinct in a dangerous situation. Courage means overcoming that fear and going into battle. Who then would not be afraid? And who would not have committed some transgression that worried him when his life – merits versus demerits – hangs in the balance?

And yet, here is the Torah mandating in clear language that these four categories of soldiers should return to the safety of their home. You can imagine thousands of soldiers streaming homeward, this one claiming that he has planted a vineyard, the other happily telling everyone of his engagement, and the

---

2. Students of Torah will know that Rashi brings two opinions that explain *afraid or fainthearted*. R' Akiva states that it is to be understood literally – a man who by nature is fearful, and cannot bear seeing weapons drawn; whereas R' Yosi HaGlili says that it refers to a man who is scared that he had committed a transgression. Either way, whatever the cause of his fear, home he must go.

third sheepishly admitting that he is scared. Any veteran battle-scarred soldier will tell you that *everyone* is scared before a battle. He would stand in disbelief at the sight of an army sending its fighting-force home because they have built nice new homes and haven't yet affixed the *mezuzos,* or because (voice lowered) they admit their fear. He would ask in stupefied amazement, "And you expect to win this war? Why don't you just tell the enemy to take possession of your land?! You are handing them victory on a velvet cushion!"

Now put yourself in the position of the enemy. These battle-hardened, granite-headed professional soldiers, who wear the shrunken skulls of their victims around their metal studded belts, who are as tough as rusty nails and as merciless as cold-eyed alligators, watch uncomprehendingly through their binoculars as the Jewish soldiers pack their bags to leave, wishing one another mazel tov on their new house and vineyard, eager to leave the dangerous battle area before the first fearful arrow flies in their direction. They watch, and they cannot comprehend. What do you think – that they would be so impressed by Jewish compassion, so overwhelmed by Torah values, that they would forgo victory in admiration? They would not believe their luck! For sure they would swoop on the decimated ranks with unmitigated glee, eager to snatch their victory.

And yet, despite the voluntary disbanding of their fighting force, the Commander of this unique strategy promises victory. *For Hashem, your G-d, is the One Who goes with you, to fight for you with your enemies, to save you* (Devarim 20:4).

One could confidently surmise that no nation in the world adopts this tactic in their battle plan and certainly not if they actually want to win. Yet, here we see written this precise instruction, clearly stated in the official constitution. Moshe himself would never have enacted such a law, a law that no army in the world possesses, and Moshe himself could never, or would never promise victory under any circumstances, let alone after instructing ninety percent of the army to return home. All because they had planted a vineyard, or they were scared! Only the Supreme Controller of all mankind would include such a law – as a demonstration to the whole world that it is indeed Hashem, the G-d of Israel, Who is the One Who goes with them, to fight their enemies and save His people. Then and always.

TWENTY-FIVE
More Mitzvos from Hashem

Imagine that you are planning a vacation. Two weeks away from home. A time to relax, switch off, recharge your batteries, see new sights, new experiences, become inspired. What could be better? Practical common sense would dictate that you secure your home before leaving for your destination in the sun. Cancel the newspaper, ask a kindly neighbor to push letters through your mailbox, perhaps set the Shabbos clock to switch a couple of lights on and off to give the house an appearance of being occupied. You would not want the longed-for vacation of your dreams to metamorphose into a living nightmare. You want to ensure that your home and possessions are safe and sound in your absence and that when you return, everything will be exactly as you left it, apart from the fruit bowl with the wrinkled apples that you forgot to eat.

What would you do if you had the misfortune of living in a rough neighborhood? All around you live not kindly, sweet-natured, honest citizens, but conniving, thieving, surly criminals, jealous of your successful farm, envious of your comfortable home. They proudly boast that there is no lock they cannot open, no security device beyond their nimble fingers. Fixing notices on your gate, "Beware the Ferocious Dog," will make them giggle;

attaching signs to your boundary, "Danger – electrocuted fence," will make them guffaw with unrestrained cynical laughter. Nothing will deter these determined burglars.

As your vacation approaches, the smirking neighbors nonchalantly inquire with feigned friendliness, "Ho there, Moshe, soon time for your vacation – when exactly are you leaving? We can't wait to wave you off!" What would happen if somehow they had discovered your precise date and time of departure, planned time of return – oh no! How secure would you be as your taxi arrives to transport you to the airport? How safe would you feel as you spy furtive evil, envious, wicked eyes peering at your retreating home from behind dark curtains?!

This exactly was the Jewish Nation's situation three times a year, as they prepared to embark on their thrice-yearly pilgrimage to Jerusalem. Except that it was worse. The non-Jewish countries that surrounded their country on three sides were always hostile (the Mediterranean on the West caused them no problem). Nothing has changed. As it is now, so it was always. A solitary sheep surrounded by hungry, hostile, heartless wolves, ready and eager to pounce. Every non-Jew knew precisely when the Jews would set out for Jerusalem. Everyone had access to Jewish calendars. Then, as now, anyone could walk (figuratively, in the former case) into a Jewish bookstore and purchase a *luach*. The festivals are all there, precisely. And because we Jews are such kindly and trusting people, we produce *"heimishe* directories" where all Shabbos-observing families (and three-time-a-year pilgrims) proudly present their names, addresses, telephone numbers, and wives' maiden names. All available from your friendly bookstore, happy to serve anyone. So the *goyim* have it all. Armed with a *luach* and a phone directory, they have all they need. Can't wait to see you go. Have a great holiday! Hee-hee!

Then it gets worse. Presumably, in the interest of safety, some men will remain behind to guard the border. Does it not stand to reason? Have we not heard of shuls in these uncertain times operating a "security rotation," where valiant members stand guard outside, ensuring that the shul is safe at all times? Would the Jewish People not behave with similar caution when everyone streams to Jerusalem, three times a year?

The answer is no. *Three times a year all your males shall appear before the Lord Hashem, the G-d of Israel* (*Shemos* 34:23). All means all. No one would guard the borders, the vulnerable farms, the delectable vineyards, the defenseless flocks and herds, the tempting farmhouses – all would remain completely undefended, three times a year, for approximately two weeks each time. No system of legislation anywhere in the world has this requirement together with its inbuilt guarantee. For good reason.

A recipe for disaster? Not exactly. The very next verse in the Torah makes a bold promise. *For I shall banish nations before you, and broaden your boundary; no man will covet your land when you go up to appear before Hashem, your G-d, three times a year* (ibid. 34:24).

Now who exactly is making this promise? Who could make a promise of this magnitude? We can remember Yom Kippur 1973 when hostile neighbors took advantage of the paucity of border guards on that Holy Day to invade Israel. And here is the Torah mandating total attendance at the Temple in Jerusalem, promising that no one would entertain the thought that must have occupied their minds the rest of the year. Who would make a promise like that – who has the capacity and capability to fulfill a promise on which the security and very existence of the Jewish Nation depends? It could not be Moshe Rabbeinu – he only lived 120 years, and never set foot into the Promised Land. And he had no power whatsoever to influence people's minds. No human being can influence someone else's mind – particularly for hundreds of years into the future, and especially the mind of someone he doesn't know. "I hereby promise that from next Rosh Hashanah until the Rosh Hashanah afterward, not a single person will want to smoke." Now that is some prediction – try it and see if it works. I doubt that the tobacco industry will spend sleepless nights worrying.

If no one could make this promise, and certainly no one in his right mind would dare to promise something over which he has no control, which can spell the doom of the people he loves, then the conclusion is blatantly clear. Only the great, supernatural G-d could enact and implement this law, and guarantee the promise integral to its fulfillment.

The mitzvah of *bris milah* is precious to the Jewish People. It is given as an example of a mitzvah which was accepted with happiness from its very inception, and continues to be fulfilled with joy (*Shabbos* 130a). Experience shows that even those with limited mitzvah observance are stringent in their adherence of this particular mitzvah.

Whoever has attended a *bris* will know that it is not an experience for the fainthearted. The eight-day-old baby is brought to the ceremony on a decorative cushion. Eight-day-old babies look fragile, diminutive, defenseless. Tiny! The *mohel*, with great skill and confidence, disrobes the unsuspecting little child and with consummate skill and aplomb, performs a delicate operation under the vigilant scrutiny of countless eyes. In two minutes, the operation is completed, baby cleaned and swaddled, and placed back on the cushion – the proud recipient of a brand-new name and copious blessings. The cause for trepidation for the fainthearted is the sight of blood. Perforce, the removal of skin-tissue results in the rupture of blood vessels, with attendant bleeding. The skillful bandaging of the *mohel* staunches the flow of blood, allowing the clotting process to proceed, expediting the healing process.

There are many people who aspire to perform the mitzvah of *milah*, but a single worry impedes their ambition. The worry of what would happen if something goes wrong! Once the knife cuts, how would you be certain that the bleeding will stop? What would happen if it didn't? Little babies are fragile – how would you dare to initiate a surgical process whose consequences are unpredictable? Who will guarantee that the baby will survive? You are at liberty to risk your own life – but who would mandate a surgical procedure some four thousand years ago, when nothing was known of the coagulation process? And why on the eighth day specifically?

Medical experts tell us that the system of blood clotting, or coagulation, depends on certain types of proteins, called platelets, which are produced by the liver. These materials, known by the Roman numerals I-XIII (1-13) work in sequence (together with various enzymes) until a substance called fibrin is formed. In the first days after birth the liver is not yet sufficiently developed to produce the proteins vital for coagulation. Physiologically, until the eighth day, the liver slowly develops, until on the eighth day itself, it is mature enough to fulfill its role to create the clots necessary to stop the bleeding (Ayala Abrahamov MD, Senior Professor of Pediatrics at the Faculty of Medicine at the Hebrew University of Jerusalem in her article, *Problems with Blood Clotting and Bleeding in Newborns*, quoted in *The Coming Revolution* by Zamir Cohen).

Here's another astounding bit of information, also included in *The Coming Revolution*; in June 2000 a new edition of the best-seller *None of These Diseases* by Dr. S.I. McMillen noted enthusiastically that in the first days of life, the newborn faces a serious dearth of blood-clotting substances; whereas after the eighth day, the level of clotting material – prothrombin – in the blood reaches its lifetime average of 100 percent. However, just before the eighth day, the amount of blood-clotting material increases rapidly, until on the eighth day itself, it is 110 percent of the norm!

In other words, only on the eighth day of life do blood-clotting materials reach their all-time high – well beyond the amount that will accompany a normal human being for the rest of his life.

As mentioned, the mitzvah of *bris milah* was given to our forefather Avraham nearly four thousand years ago (3,729 years at the time of writing). We can be quite sure that the intricacies of blood coagulation, and its mechanism and chemical sequence, were unknown at that time. No one who loved Jewish children would give instructions to perform a sensitive operation on a tiny baby, just-about born, that could have the severest of consequences. The only One who would, or could, is the Creator of all flesh. Only the Designer and Manufacturer of human beings has the ability, the knowledge, and the authority to give this command, and guarantee its safety.

Another, perhaps less well-known, example of a mitzvah which carries a discernible sign of the Divine is that which is mentioned in *Parshas Mishpatim* (*Shemos* 21:37): if a person steals an ox or sheep, and then slaughters or sells it, he must repay five oxen for each ox, and four sheep for each sheep. Rashi explains, quoting *Chazal* (*Maseches Bava Kamma* 79b), that the Torah gives consideration to human dignity. When stealing a cow – an animal of substantial girth – the animal trots after the thief on its own four sturdy legs. However, as those in the sheep-stealing fraternity will attest, when stealing a sheep, the animal is placed around the neck of the thief as he surreptitiously tiptoes away from the scene of the crime. The indignity suffered by the thief by having a sheep around his shoulders is noted by the Torah, and is sufficient to mitigate his punishment so that he repays only four times the value of the sheep to the owner, as opposed to five times the value of an ox for a similar crime.

Put into a modern context, the sensitivity of the Torah is brought into clear focus. Imagine a thief who gains his illegal wages by climbing into houses and stealing their contents. On one occasion, he scaled a ladder, gained entry through an open window, and emptied the contents of the owner's jewelry box into a sack. Upon descending the ladder, the sack slung over his back, he was welcomed by the wide arms of a policeman waiting at ground level. The hapless thief was deposited in a jail cell, awaiting trial. At the court hearing, the judge heard the evidence – as clear as a sunny day – and before passing sentence, asked if anyone had anything to say in his defense. From the gallery arose a plaintive voice, "Yes, Your Honor!" A little old lady stood up and said, "Oh please, Judge, don't be hard on poor Jimmy. He's really a kind boy, and was only trying to earn a living. And in any case, that sack with all the jewelry inside was really dirty – it stained his shirt something terrible. It was a clean shirt, too, when he put it on and it took me ages to remove the stain. Poor, poor Jimmy, having to walk around with a dirty shirt – such a shame – Your Honor, please have mercy on Jimmy!"

Who do you think is the old lady in this example? Who is the only person in the world who would feel this degree of compassion for a thief – only his mother. A mother is a mother, and will love her son no matter what, and will find redeeming features where others will see none.

The Torah has pity on the sheep-thief. It is Hashem Who made the thief, cares for him, feeds him, wants his good, and feels his indignity. It is only Hashem, the Author of the Torah, who loves the thief more than ten mothers who would show compassion for the soiled collar. It is a safe assumption that in a review of all countries' legislations, nowhere will be found that the soiled clothing of the poor thief is grounds for mitigation of punishment for stealing. *Hashem Levado*! Only Hashem, the loving Father, would include this statute of consideration for His eternal legislation.

TWENTY-SIX
The Future Revealed

Wealth has always held a fascination, whether it is the delectable thought of possessing limitless riches, or simply the pressing need for cash. Many countries organize a form of national lottery in which for a modest investment one can purchase a ticket, which if it holds the lucky numbers, can procure for the owner tens – sometimes hundreds – of millions. Being the possessor of a ticket allows you to dream – how you will keep your sudden wealth a secret; how you will distribute huge sums to your nearest and dearest without revealing your identity; will you continue working, or will you sit in shul behind bulging bags of cash, the answer to every *meshulach's* dream? It is a tantalizing dream, and the chance to dream itself is worth the small purchase price.

Is it possible to know the selected numbers in advance? Has anyone ever chosen the winning numbers (in the systems that allow the contestant to choose his own numbers) based on a revelation? Apparently not, otherwise the same person would win multiple times. The very efficacy of games of chance is precisely that – no one *has* prior knowledge of the results, nor *can have* knowledge. It is purely a matter of chance – or as Jewish people would say, *hashgachah* – that will decide the winner.

Interestingly, there are many groups of people who should have access to those elusive numbers. Every fairground boasts a tent in which a lady, wearing large earrings and a bright *tichel*, sits hunched over an inverted goldfish bowl and for a set fee will reveal your future destiny. The higher the fee, the rosier the future! Attending a fairground is a questionable practice for a Jew – and asking the said lady for your future is forbidden by the Torah, but still, there are many groups of people who claim to have access to the future. There are clairvoyants, soothsayers, astrologers, people who communicate with spirits, folk who read tea leaves, palm readers, witch doctors and stargazers, people who claim to know the future from the shape of molten lead dropped into water, or from the flights of birds – surely there must be one of these hopeful people who can successfully probe the secrets of the future and become wealthy in the process?

In contrast, the Torah, while prohibiting occult practices, assures Jewish people that they can have, and will have, access to the future events through the medium of prophecy. *When you come to the land that G-d your Lord is giving you, do not learn to do the revolting practices of those nations. Among you there shall not be found anyone who passes his son or daughter through fire, who practices stick divination, who divines auspicious times, who divines by omens* (superstitions), *who practices witchcraft, who uses incantations, who consults mediums and oracles, or who attempts to communicate with the dead…what G-d has given to you is totally different. In your midst* (the Land of Israel) *G-d will set up for you a prophet like me from among your brethren, and it is to him that you must listen* (*Shoftim* 18:9-15).

The privilege of prophecy was bestowed on the Jews as a result of the trepidation they felt when they themselves heard the voice of Hashem thundering from Mount Sinai.

This is the result of the request that you made of G-d your Lord at Chorev (Mount Sinai) *on the day of assembly* (giving of the Torah) *when you said, "We cannot listen to the voice of G-d our Lord anymore. We cannot look at this great fire anymore. We do not want to die!" G-d then said to me* (Moshe), *"They have spoken well. I will set up a prophet for them from among their brethren, just as you are. I will place My word in his mouth and he will declare to them all that I command him"* (ibid. 18:16-18).

The Torah commands us to listen to the instructions of a prophet, and recounts the punishment for failing to do so. Conversely, there's a prohibition against pretending to make declarations in G-d's name when no communication was received, or speaking in the name of other gods. How then will people know who is a genuine prophet? The Torah poses this question and gives a definitive answer. *You may ask yourselves, "How shall we recognize that a declaration was not spoken by G-d?" If the prophet predicts something in G-d's name and the prediction does not materialize or come true, then the message was not spoken by G-d. The prophet has spoken deceitfully, and you must not fear him* (ibid. 18:21-22).

The words, *I will set up a prophet from amongst them just as you are... I will place My word in his mouth...* are a stupendous claim, unique in the annals of history. No human can place words in someone else's mouth. You cannot program a human to say what you want him to say. It has been tried countless times. Imagine you are collecting charitable funds. Sitting across the table is the writer of the check. He sits, hand poised while deep in thought. Now is your chance! Beam into his mind with all the powers of your concentration: "One…million…dollars." Then he writes, "eighteen dollars"! No one can control another person's thoughts, or another person's speech. Bearing in mind that many times genuine prophets had to deliver messages that were antagonistic, unpopular, and full of censure (think of Yonah, Moshe, Yirmiyahu, Mordechai), words that they themselves would not have chosen to say; it is clear that the source of the message was not of their making. Rather, it was an outside powerful source that predicated that these messages will be given and fulfilled – that source was Hashem.

The prophecies that we read in Tanach are similar to the wonders and kindness that we experience in our bodies. They are so numerous that we so easily take them for granted. But, just like we are awed when we take a closer look at the magnificent design of our bodies, so a more detailed observation of a few prophecies recorded in the Torah will allow us to appreciate the amazing phenomenon of prophecy.

Our father Avraham was the recipient of striking prophecies that could not have been predicted by anyone on the basis of natural expectation, yet their impact is experienced to this very day.

I will make you into a great nation. I will bless you and make you great. You shall become a blessing. I will bless those who bless you, and he who curses you, I will curse. All the families of the earth will be blessed through you (Bereishis 12:1-3). Here is a man – already a seventy-five-year-old senior who has yet to have descendants – with his wife, being told to relocate to a place where he is currently unknown, with the promise that he will be the progenitor of a great nation, and he will be so famous that his name will be revered universally. Now, all of us know that however much we like someone and wish to make them happy, we just cannot promise that they will develop into a great nation or become famous throughout the world. You can hope it, wish it, but you cannot promise it. Ever. And certainly not a promise that will endure for thousands of years!

Yet here we are, some 3,775 years after the promise was made to Avraham, identifiably his sons, members of a nation which, despite many people's best efforts, refuses to disappear, and who are prominently center players on the world stage. And look around. The Christians respect their Abes, the Mohammedans revere their Ibrahims, and we seek to emulate our Avraham. Who could have predicted that the life's work of one man, teaching the truths of Monotheism, would be the primary source and inspiration for thousands of millions of believers in G-d throughout the millennia? That prophecy, written in the Torah some 3,330 years ago, is alive and well today – witnessed by the whole world. Who could make such a promise? Only G-d.

Then we have the claim of the Jews to the Land of Israel. There is an interesting phenomenon experienced by so many Jewish people when they visit Israel. Everyone feels at home in the country of their origin – comfortable in their surroundings, familiar with the culture, fluent in the language – yet when they arrive in Eretz Yisrael, there is an immediate affinity, a tangible feeling of coming home. Seasoned travelers will have witnessed the enthusiasm that natives of a country demonstrate when the plane lands safely on the runway of their beloved land. That same enthusiasm – perhaps even greater – is evidenced as the flight to Israel nears its destination. Necks are craned, noses are pressed against the window, anxious, eager, excited to see the first glimpse of the coastline of…Eretz Yisrael! "It's there! I can see it!" Hearts beat faster, blood runs quicker, tiredness dissipates, excitement rises…Eretz Yisrael! Our Home. This sense of homecoming is as strong today as it ever was – and will always be. From where does that powerful and compelling feeling emanate?

After Lot left him, Hashem said to Avram, *Raise your eyes, and from the place where you are now standing, look to the north, to the south, to the east, and to the west. For all the land you see, I will give to you and to your offspring forever.* Come what may, whatever the circumstances, through thick and thin – it is a promise. Even a cursory glance at the turbulence of world politics will demonstrate that nothing is stable and nothing is static. Little over a hundred years ago, Britain prided itself on an empire over which the sun never set. Spanning the globe, from east to west, "Britannia ruled the waves." Political forces, social pressures, nationalistic aspirations, the desire for independence – and a hundred years later it has all changed. New alliance, changed names, population shifts, and the world map is unrecognizable.

Just over five hundred years ago, virtually no one in the world would have heard of the name America. That name was first used on a map in the year 1507. Just three hundred years ago that country was a sparsely populated British colony with a neighboring French colony called Canada to the north. Today, the USA and Canada form the most powerful union of countries in the world, but are populated by a polyglot of peoples from around the globe.

Imagine saying, "There will always be a Babylonian Kingdom"; "The Ottoman Empire will endure forever"; "The Romans are eternal"; "The Byzantine Dynasty is unbreakable." No one says those things, and for good reason. The last person to attempt to establish a German empire that would endure for 1,000 years is the man everyone wants to forget, and his evil empire lasted just twelve miserable years.

A prophecy and promise was given to our father Avraham that the small piece of land on which he dwelt would remain with his family "*l'olam*" – forever; and throughout every political turbulence, empire-come-and-go, invasions, and exiles, there it is, as it always has been, will always be, the land that the Jews call home.

TWENTY-SEVEN
Prophecies That Defy the Odds

No one wishes to have a monopoly on suffering, yet of all the nations of the world, it would appear that the Jewish Nation has been singled out for special treatment. Special in privileges, and special in retribution.

The Torah gives vivid and detailed prophecies – graphic descriptions – of the results of obedience to the dictates of Hashem's Torah, and conversely the consequences of disobedience. Should anyone ever ask, "Why do so many bad things happen to the Jewish People – where was G-d in Auschwitz?" direct them to open up a Chumash and draw their attention to the relevant passages. Twice every day, Jews are commanded to recite the three paragraphs of the Shema. The second paragraph describes clearly the formula of reward and punishment that are the consequences of listening to Hashem's commands, or failure to do so.[1]

---

1. *If you are careful to pay heed to My commandments which I am prescribing to you today, and if you love Hashem your G-d with all your heart and soul (then G-d has made this promise)... I will grant you fall and spring, rains in your land at their proper time so that you will have ample harvest of grain, oil, and wine... you will eat and be satisfied. Be careful that your heart not be tempted to go astray and worship other gods... G-d's anger will then be directed against you, and He will lock up the skies so that there will not be any rain. The land will not give forth its crops, and you will rapidly vanish from the good land that G-d is giving you...* (Devarim 11:13-18).

More detailed and graphic accounts of reward and punishment are contained in two key passages of the Torah. The first is in *Bechukosai* (26:3-46) where the Jewish People are promised security, prosperity, agricultural abundance, and military superiority for adhering to Hashem's commands; whereas a lackluster and lackadaisical attitude toward mitzvos will result in reciprocal lack of protection from Hashem and exile from their land amidst great personal suffering. What is particularly noteworthy is that all these dire predictions – forty-nine in number – were given to them before they had even set foot in their Promised Land.

The second passage is toward the end of the Torah in *Ki Savo* (28:1-68). There, blessings of peace and prosperity are vouchsafed to the Jewish People for obedience, but ninety-eight separate punishments are detailed as the consequence for the lack of obedience; invasion by cruel, heartless oppressors; the horrors of starvation and disease caused by siege and famine; human cannibalism and captivity – all dire predictions too awful to imagine. Except that each and every one of them was fulfilled to the last grim detail in the twin calamities of the destruction of the First Temple by the Babylonians, and the Second Temple by the Romans, as well as in subsequent periods of persecution.

There is something unique about these *pesukim* that delineates the consequences of our loyalty to our Divine mission; they are exceedingly detailed and precise. Vague predictions are easy enough to make; *everything will be good, all* brachos – or – *be good otherwise who knows what could happen, the future does not look rosy... But to state categorically, G-d will bring upon you a nation from afar, from the end of the earth, swooping down like an eagle. It will be a nation whose language you do not understand, a sadistic nation... You will bring much seed out to the field, but the locust will devour the crop and you will bring little back; you will plant vineyards and work hard, but the worms will eat the grapes... G-d will bring you back to Egypt in ships along the way that I promised you would never see again. You will try to sell yourselves as slaves and maids, but no one will want to buy you (Parshas Ki Savo)* – that level of detail can only be promised by the One with a hand on the controls of history.

The Torah even predicts the reaction of the nations of the world to the unprecedented display of fury directed to the Jews, and their instinctive understanding of the case. *All the nations will ask, "Why did G-d do this to the Land, what was the reason for this great display of anger?" They shall answer, "It is because they abandoned the covenant that G-d, Lord of their fathers, made with them when He brought them out of Egypt – they went and served foreign gods, bowing down to them..."* (Devarim 29:23-25).

In the long list of features that are unique to the Jewish People, the plethora of detailed prophecies that plot the future destiny of this special nation stand high on the chart. Weather forecasts based on a wealth of data obtained from satellite and wind-directions are the limit of human predicting capabilities. Not a single human being in his right mind will publish forty-nine plus ninety-eight detailed forewarnings about matters over which he has no control. Why open yourself up to ridicule and refutation?

Only the Torah, authored by the Controller of all human destiny, could disclose the future course of the history of His people based on the adherence to His laws.

But in the tragic there is magic. In the midst of the dire predictions, where one might think that the disappearance or annihilation of the Jews is the sure consequence of the relentless persecution so predicted – just there – the Torah issues a guarantee that promises that our precious nation will never disappear. *Thus even when they are in their enemies' land I will not grow so disgusted with them nor so tired of them that I would destroy them and break My covenant with them, since I am G-d their Lord (Vayikra 26:44).*

This affirmation of indestructibility is remarkable for several reasons. Firstly, it is unlikely that any other nation in the world has been so relentlessly persecuted, maligned, expelled, and ostracized, or has the unwelcome privilege of having endured so many attempts to eradicate, annihilate, and exterminate every single member from the face of earth.

Secondly, the Torah gives us the least optimum chances for survival. Consider a situation where a particular species is endangered. The majestic golden eagle, once a common sight soaring over the hills and glens of Scotland, became a vulnerable species almost to the point of extinction. Naturalists and conservationists joined forces to declare large acres of rural Scotland out of bounds to the public, to enable the surviving eagles to breed and replenish undisturbed. Due to the protective measures put in place by the concerned authorities, the number of golden eagles increased, eggs of future generations were laid and hatched with impunity, and once again, the royal eagles rule the skies. The last thing in the world you would advise is to disperse the poor wee chickens around the world while leaving them prey to the dangers of the wild. Now compare that to the following two statements made in the Torah: *Where you were once as numerous as the stars of the sky, the survivors among you will be few in number* (Devarim 28:62), and: *I will scatter you among the nations, and keep the sword drawn against you* (*Vayikra* 26:33). Few in number and scattered around the world is a sure formula for quick disappearance – all the more given the hostility that will meet them everywhere. And yet – with all the odds stacked against us, with every disadvantage, with every possible handicap – the promise of endurance forever is given as a guarantee. Who could give and who could fulfill that impossible feat? Only Hashem.

In the annals of history – and in particular Jewish history, where persecution was no stranger – there can be no period more painful than the Holocaust. In the fanatical hatred of Amalek's modern descendants and their systematic desire to destroy the whole of world Jewry in which they were 33 percent successful, practically the whole of European Jewry was annihilated. The statistics of the horror almost defy comprehension. Over a six-year period, approximately six million Jewish people were killed. Six years is 2,190 days. Imagine a thriving community of three thousand Jewish souls; men, women, and children; with schools, yeshivos, *kollelim*, shops, and shuls; with a whole infrastructure of *rabbanim*, organizations, and *gemachim*. A beautiful community – a microcosm of the Jewish world. Now imagine a community like that destroyed on each and every one of those 2,190 days. Three thousand per day for 2,190 days is the total of Jewish victims of the Holocaust. Indeed, we can only echo the pain of Yirmiyahu where he laments, *Behold and see – is there any pain like my pain which befell me; which Hashem has afflicted me on the day of His burning wrath* (*Eichah* 1:12).

In that terrible and unprecedented conflagration was destroyed almost every European yeshivah; Mir, Slabodka, Telshe, Grodno, Radin, Baranovitch, Ponevezh, Lomzhe, Bialystok, Kamenitz, Kletzk, Slonim, Kelm, Kobrin, Lubavitch, Radomsk, Lublin, Kishinev, Charnowitz, Vizhnitz, Pressburg, Berlin, Heide; all bastions of Jewish learning fell to the Nazi hordes. Europe was the reservoir of Torah scholarship where for over one thousand years, yeshivos and Torah study flourished. Rashi, the *Ba'alei Tosfos, Rishonim, Acharonim* – the whole body of Torah resided and resounded in Europe. When Europe was destroyed, its Torah citadels were usually the first victims of the vicious anti-Jewish sentiment. To any contemporary witness of that horrifying era, it looked like the end of Torah learning. True, there were fledgling Torah institutions in England, the USA, and Israel, but they were few in number and struggling to stay afloat. The prognosis looked grim – the great Torah bastions of Europe were gone; any survivors were gasping for breath, happy to just be alive; Torah learning in the free world was nascent and frail – how could Torah survive?

The answer is a single verse in the Torah.

With amazing foresight, in the midst of the passage foretelling the negative consequences of turning to foreign gods, the Torah declares, *It shall be that when many evils and distresses come upon it – then this song shall speak up before it as a witness, for it shall not be forgotten from the mouth of its offspring* (Devarim 31:31). On those fateful words, *for it shall not be forgotten*, the great commentator Rashi, quoting the Talmud in *Shabbos* (138b), states, "This is a promise to Israel that Torah will never be completely forgotten." So there we have it – a Divine promise that Torah will have continuity. Never ever, despite the fiercest opposition and unprecedented persecutions, will Torah be forgotten. Torah study will endure and flourish. Like Hashem, like the people of Israel, Torah is eternal.

And those of us who have merited to be born after this most recent period of destruction can see with our own eyes the fulfillment of that cast-iron prophecy. Go to Israel, go to America both South and North, go to England, to Australia, to Europe – even, unbelievably, to the epicenter of the previous evil empire – and see yeshivos, *kollelim*, schools, seminaries, and *chadarim* flourishing and thriving, proliferating and multiplying *bli ayin hara*! Who could have thought, who could have dreamt, that from the ashes of Europe could grow a forest of Torah, strong and vibrant, alive and pulsating – only Hashem could promise a rebirth of such supernatural magnitude and effect its fulfillment.

TWENTY-EIGHT
The Most Unlikely

In the fulfillment of the prophecy that Torah study would endure, and in the rebirth of Torah observance in the United States, Hashem chose two of the most unlikely candidates for the leading roles.

The Satmar Rav, Rav Yoel Teitelbaum *zt"l*, was widely recognized as a *gaon* and tzaddik even before World War I. With Hashem's mercy, he miraculously survived the Holocaust, eventually settling in Williamsburg, New York. When the rebbe first came to the United States, it was almost unheard of for anyone to wear a *shtreimel* in the street on Shabbos. The rebbe ignored this reality and immediately wore his *shtreimel*, as well as his complete Shabbos attire, in public, as he was accustomed in Europe before the war. Less than two decades later, the streets of Williamsburg swarmed with hundreds of chassidim proudly wearing their *shtreimlach* on Shabbos and Yom Tov.

When trying to understand the scale of improbability of a *chassidishe rebbe* fomenting a spiritual revolution in America, one has to understand the extent to which the rebbe stood alone in almost every aspect of his religious viewpoints. The story is recounted how on one Shabbos, the rebbe was walking, accompanied by the Nanasher Rebbe, Rabbi Zvi Avigdor Fekete *zt"l*, and the *gabbai*, R' Yosef Ashkenazi, who did not yet wear his *shtreimel* on the street. Across the road, a group of young, noisy, burly non-Jews gesticulated toward them, bursting out in raucous laughter. The rebbe paid them no attention. R' Yosef Ashkenazi could not constrain himself. "The rebbe saw that vulgar laughter? One cannot walk with a *shtreimel* in the street without provoking this type of a reaction!"

Immediately, the rebbe retorted with a serene smile on his face, "You really believe they were laughing at the two of us who were wearing *shtreimlach*? I would say that they were laughing at you, because they see two *Yidden* wearing *shtreimlach*, and the third one is not..."

If the rebbe felt himself leading a one-man army in his fight to establish a community willing to adhere to the traditional standards of a pre-war European model, whether in kashrus, education, and *tznius*, nothing could compare to the opposition that the rebbe encountered toward his stance on Zionism. Before the war, the rebbe had been a determined opponent of secular Zionism and the dangers it posed to the Jewish people. As soon as he arrived in America, he realized to his dismay that the majority of Torah Jewry in the United States were favorably disposed to the creation of a Jewish state. Although many Torah sages of previous generations had shared the fierce opposition to modern Zionism and any Jewish statehood before the coming of Mashiach, nonetheless, the trauma and horror of the Holocaust changed the climate of opinion radically. The personal suffering endured by so many at the hands of the nations created a surge of yearning for an independent State of Israel that they could call home. When the Zionist dream became a reality in 1947, a tidal wave of euphoria swept through the Jewish Nation. To the hundreds of thousands of survivors broken in body and spirit, the creation of a Jewish homeland, where a Jew could live free and unoppressed, was a balm to their shattered souls. Everyone was a Zionist! Elation, hope, and tolerance – everyone was swept along by the wave of popular emotion.

Except one man, and a pitifully small group of loyal supporters. To stand against the tide of public feeling in those days, to insist that nothing had changed, to maintain that Zionism was just another false Messiah sent to test our people – was a stance that singled the rebbe out for the fiercest condemnation, opposition, and even ridicule from the whole spectrum of Judaism. At that painful period, when he was a lone voice against the world, struggling to even gather a *minyan* for regular *tefillos*, the chances of him establishing a thriving community and changing the face of American Jewry would have been measured at an absolute zero.

Now turn the clock forward just six decades and survey the scene. *Chassidus* is arguably the fastest growing sector of world Jewry at large, and American Jewry specifically. The Satmar *chassidus* boasts tens of thousands of loyal followers, and the warm climate of acceptance that the Satmar Rav merited later in his life encouraged many rebbes to establish centers in America to an extent unimaginable two or three generations ago.

Good things happen through good people without a doubt, but to arrive at a situation where in modern America – the land of freedom and assimilation – thousands of families proudly identify, visibly and ideologically, with full-blooded *chassidus*, is nothing short of miraculous. And the fulfillment of a prophecy recorded in an eternal Torah some 3,330 years ago.

Meanwhile, in the non-chassidic sector (popularly known as "*yeshivish*" or "*Litvish*"), a wonder of similar proportions was transforming the American scene. What the Satmar Rav was to the *chassidishe* world, Harav Aharon Kotler *zt"l* was to the yeshivah world. Rav Kotler was a man of fiery conviction, a man who had already founded and led a yeshivah in Kletzk, Poland, and was renowned for his passion for Torah and his deep and penetrating *shiurim*. But that he could transplant that zeal and conviction to a barren American landscape was unimaginable.

The scope of the challenge is best expressed by Rabbi Yitzchok Berkovitz, in his comprehensive biography, *The Legacy of Maran Rav Aharon Kotler*.

"There was a major difference between the situation in Europe and that which the Rosh Yeshivah found in America. In Europe, the groundwork for Torah dissemination was there. The concept of learning Torah for its own sake…was ingrained in European *bnei yeshivah* from the time of Rav Chaim Volozhin, the Vilna Gaon and before…

"Not so in America, where the spirit of pragmatism, '*tachlis*' (goal), and career reigned supreme. Struggling immigrants wanted financial security for their children – and that meant long-term secular studies. Religious parents, of course, wanted *Yiddishkeit* for their children too…and to that end they formed and sent their children to yeshivos. But the goal of financial betterment and secular education was ever-present, and yeshivos, if they wished to keep their students, had to accommodate that goal. Mornings and part of the afternoons were spent in yeshivah; evenings and nights saw an exodus to the city colleges.

"The concept and practical possibility of devoting many years in yeshivah and *kollel* to total absorption in learning *Torah lishmah* to become a great Torah scholar, simply did not exist… Yeshivah learning was understood and accepted only in terms of what one will *do* with his Torah, not for its inherent value.

"The Rosh Yeshivah was terribly concerned about the situation – concerned but not at all worried. He set about doing what he knew had to be done, preparing himself to suffer and to sacrifice for the sake of Torah – and placed his trust in the One Who guaranteed His people that Torah will never be forgotten. He lived with the prophecy of the guarantee of Torah's survival and endurance on his lips. Indeed, the Rosh Yeshivah had to counter opposition, apathy, and often bitter antagonism, even from religious Jews."

Rav Aharon Kotler's assertion that Torah has a future in America, as unlikely as it appeared, was vindicated in full measure. Today, thousands of *kollel* men fill Lakewood, a powerhouse of Torah learning, which in turn, has spawned numerous satellite *kollelim* in the USA and around the world.

The transformation of America from a spiritual wasteland to a fertile, fruitful plain where countless yeshivos produce *bachurim* dedicated to Torah learning at the highest level is in no small measure due to the example, efforts, and idealism of a supremely inspired *gadol*. From where did he get his inspiration? From Hashem's promise that Torah would never be forgotten. The scenario that presented the least chance of success was precisely the one with which Hashem alone effected the greatest fulfillment of His promise. *Ein Od Milvado.*

TWENTY-NINE

The New Car

Acquiring a new car is always a pleasure. The look is clean, the lines are smooth, the tires are pristine and firm, and the car's emblem gives a confident feeling. Although strange at first, the controls become familiar with the passage of time. People's admiring comments add to the appreciation. "Nice car you've got there"; "*Tis'chadesh* on your new car!"; "Fabulous car, that one…" As new features are discovered – climate control, assisted parking, keyless locking, lane-keeping aid, cruise control – so does the recognition of the level of design and planning that has produced this vehicle.

The seats are comfortable – soft leather, and are adjustable by the press of a button. The gentle turn of another knob switches on the engine, while the softest pressure on the accelerator pedal releases the handbrake. The car even has a voice! Press the button with the human profile and a mechanical monotone voice asks, "What do you want to do?" Tell the voice that you would like to access the navigation system, and it will obligingly instruct you how to proceed. Fancy talking to your car!

After the euphoria and novelty has faded somewhat, rational thoughts begin to develop. A car is a machine, designed with a singular purpose – to convey its passenger from one location to another in safety and comfort. It has an engine in which fuel is combusted, providing the energy to move pistons which in turn move rods connected to four circular rubber-covered wheels. A steering wheel permits the human driver to exercise his freedom of will to guide the vehicle in the direction of his choice, while the accelerator and break increase and inhibit the velocity. An ambient atmosphere is provided by air heaters and coolers, while an array of lights, powered by a battery, signal to the driver behind you of your desire to brake or change directions, while the twin-beams of light in front illuminate the darkness. Fuel is limited to specifics; not orange juice or dry wine or even carbonated water will provide the necessary combustion – only petroleum will suffice.

On one hand, the car is greatly appreciated. It is a marvelous machine; it enables people to undertake journeys in a fraction of the time that their great-grandfather's horse-drawn carriage could trundle along. Great-Grandpa would have marveled at the speed and comfort afforded by your car; indeed, it joins the telephone and electricity as discoveries that have transformed our lives.

On the other hand, we are aware of its limitations. When I talk to my car and it dutifully passes the pre-programmed question, "What would you like to do?" and I say, "Learn the whole of *Shas* and be an *ehrliche Yid*," the poor pre-programmed mechanical voice is flummoxed and exclaims, "Please type in the first line of your address." The car cannot climb stairs, will never smile, cannot prevent the driver hitting a brick wall, will not self-repair if scratched, or self-inflate its tires if they deflate. The windshield washer needs to be filled with soapy water, preferably with an anti-freezing additive; doors need to be manually closed; the windshield cannot see; the engine needs to be regularly serviced; and don't forget to change the oil.

Despite its limitations (it is only a machine after all), the knowledge that it was designed and crafted by a superior intelligence is axiomatic – self-evidently true. The first question asked by any car's admirer will be, "What make is it?" The question pre-supposes that no machine pops into existence by itself. The admirer, on closer scrutiny, will observe that wheels run more smoothly on rubber than on iron and that round-shaped wheels are more efficient than square ones; a toughened glass windshield gives clearer visibility than tissue paper; brakes that slow the wheels' rotation are more effective than throwing an anchor out of the window, and electrically powered blinkers are more efficient than the driver shouting out, "I'm turning right!" (given that the driver in the car behind would most likely not hear the shouts). Seeing the myriad of details, he understands instinctively that human intelligence designed it all, and his question will only be, "Which company – is it Ford, Volvo, BMW, Nissan…?" And when you respond, "Volvo V90," he will purse his lips appreciatively and say, "V90…not bad!"

If it is axiomatic that the car – with all its limitations – is the product of Mr. Skoda's brilliant team of designers, then it should be even more axiomatic that Mr. Volvo or Mr. Skoda, Henry Ford or Lord Rolls-Royce, and all the other gifted manufacturers

The New Car

of cars are, likewise, designed by a supreme intelligence. If no machine exists that either created itself, or popped into existence by random forces, then the super-super complex machine that we call a human being must obey the same criteria. A simple *kal v'chomer*.

The car's owner's manual lists in its index approximately five hundred different functions and components – hood release, seat adjustment, etc. – each of which is comprehendible and relatively simple. By contrast, a basic volume of *Principles of Anatomy and Physiology* contains some ten thousand entries in its index, from abdomen and veins to zymogenic cells, and each of the entries is complex beyond belief.

Take the previously mentioned mechanism of blood coagulation. When a pressurized blood-circulation system is punctured, a clot must form quickly to prevent the leakage of all the blood, as would happen if a plastic bottle of orange juice would spring a leak. If blood congeals in the wrong time or place, though, the clot may block circulation, with serious consequences. Furthermore, a clot has to stop bleeding all along the length of the cut, sealing it completely. Yet blood-clotting must be confined to the cut, or the entire blood system of the body might solidify, which is not conducive to a long life. Consequently, the clotting of blood must be tightly controlled so that the clot forms only when and where it is required.

"When an animal is cut, a protein called Hageman factor sticks to the surface of the cells near the wound. Bound Hageman is then cleaved by a protein called HMK to yield activated

Hageman factor. Immediately, the activated Hageman factor converts another protein, called prekallikrein, to its active form. Kallikrein helps HMK speed up the conversion of more Hageman factor to its active form. Activated Hageman factor and HMK together transform another protein called PTA to its active form. Activated PTA in turn, together with the activated form of another protein called convertin, switch a protein called Xmas factor to its active form. Finally, activated Xmas factor together with antihemophilic factor (which is itself activated by thrombin in a manner similar to that of proaccelerin) changes Stuart factor to its active form…" (Michal Behe, *Darwin's Black Box*).

The multi-staged cascade of chemical reactions requires every component of the process to be present – this one an activator, that one an accelerator, another one an inhibitor – for the whole thing to work. The absence of a single link in the chain-reaction will spell tragedy. When a *mohel* declares that a baby is yellow, he is telling us that one of the coagulatory factors has not yet been released, hence the danger in performing an operation. When said *mohel* clears the baby for a *bris*, he is informing us that a process of mind-numbing complexity is fully functioning. In the relief that follows his pronouncement, we are paying homage to the Designer of a life-saving mechanism on which our very existence depends – and therein lies the essence of a great truth.

Michal Behe, an eminent Biochemical Scientist, in his book *Darwin's Black Box* (published by The Free Press in 1996), describes the minimum criteria necessary for a machine – and in the language of biology, an organ – to function. For a system to function, it needs be irreducibly complex. That means that there is a single system composed of several well-matched, interacting parts that contribute to the basic function, in which the removal of any of the parts causes the system to effectively cease functioning. An irreducibly *complex* system cannot be produced directly by slight successive modifications of an existing system, because any deficiency to an irreducibly complex system means the system could not function. All the components must be present (as in the case of the blood-coagulation cascade) for the system to work at all.

Any system that needs all its components to work for it to perform the task is called minimal function. It must have the ability to accomplish its tasks in physically realistic circumstances. In order to lock your front door, you need a locking mechanism in the door, preferably at the edge; a groove in the doorpost; and a key to turn the lock. And don't forget the door. Every one of those components is vital and irreplaceable (irreducibly complex) and every one of the components has to function correctly for it to work at all (minimal function). If there was a door but it was too wide for the aperture in the wall, if the lock was rusted and did not turn, if the groove in the doorpost was higher than the lock's bolt, if the key did not fit the key-hole – then the whole operation could not function and you might want to think of barricading the door with your freezer to discourage unwanted visitors.

In any machine – as simple as a door lock – the absence of a single component that would render the system unusable might not be disastrous; there are alternatives and contingency plans that could be activated to guarantee security (think of an armed guard). But if life depended on the full functioning of that system, and the absence of a single component would disable the system on which life depends, then we understand well how that system must have been perfect from the very beginning.

In the same way that a cursory glance at a car will prompt the question, "That's a good car – what make is it?" similarly, even superficial knowledge of how our own bodies work will clearly convince the thinking person that we, too, have a Designer and a Master Manufacturer – *Bereishis bara Elokim.*

THIRTY
Seven Interdependent Systems

Let us not allow our familiarity with things to obscure the wonders that they contain, and our ability to see the Divine design that they demonstrate. Look at the human being (your very own self) and imagine that you are seeing it for the very first time.

Some basic facts. In order to function, the body needs bones to form the skeletal system. These bones support and protect vital organs. They give the body shape and form. But they cannot be rigid, like steel girders that support a building. They have to be jointed to allow the skeleton to adopt countless positions. To sit, stand, walk, lift, climb, stretch, kneel, bend, lie, and run – inability to move would be no fun. To move the frame, you need muscles.

You possess some 640 muscles. They are attached to the bones by connective tissue called tendons. The contraction and relaxation of muscles pulls the bones into different positions. The fingers that are clutching the pen that is writing these words are able to do their job thanks to the muscles that are pulling and positioning the bones. But what fires the muscles? For that we need the nervous system.

Think of the electrical wiring system that snakes around your house carrying electrical impulses to all the implements and lights that allow your home to function. Similarly, but vastly more complex, are the nerve fibers that carry signals from the brain. Thoughts from the brain (have you ever thought what a thought was?) trigger electro-chemical impulses that travel through the nervous system which are in turn connected to every muscle. The nervous system, vastly complex though it is, cannot function without nourishment. In common with every single one of our trillions of individual cells (each one of which is more complex than an international airport), the nervous system requires nourishment. For that we need blood.

Blood is the fluid that circulates through the heart, arteries, capillaries, and veins and constitutes the chief means of transporting oxygen and bespoke nutrients (made to order) from the digestive system throughout the body. In addition, as the chief transportation system in the body, the blood carries carbon dioxide from the cells to the lungs, it carries heat and waste products from the cells, and hormones from endocrine glands to other body cells. Besides which, it adjusts body temperature through the heat-absorbing and cooling properties of its water content. In every human being there is an estimated 60,000 miles (100,000 km) of blood veins, arteries, and capillaries – perfectly shaped, maintained (in the UK, a fifteen-mile stretch of dual carriageway was recently upgraded to motorway. It took four years and cost 183 million pounds) to deliver vital nutrients and remove waste material. The magnificent pump that propels the blood through its 60,000 miles of highways is the heart.

The heart is perfectly designed for its vital task, so that even while you are sleeping, your heart (not much larger than your fist) pumps thirty times its own weight each minute, some 3,600 gallons a day, or 2.6 million gallons (ten million liters) a year. The heart has unique properties that permit a lifetime of pumping with never a minute's rest.

All cells require oxygen to allow them to function, and the chemical reaction that occurs in cells releases carbon dioxide – which in excessive amounts is toxic to cells and must be eliminated, fast. The two systems that cooperate to supply oxygen and eliminate carbon dioxide are the heart and the lungs. The heart is the central pump, and the air intake and exhalation, in which oxygen is inhaled and carbon dioxide is expelled, are the twin lungs. As in so many of our bodies' systems, the efficient working and cooperation of heart and lungs is vital to life, as oxygen starvation or build-up of waste products can both be damaging in the extreme.

We thank Hashem for food daily. And for good reason. Food contains many nutrients, molecules needed for building new – and repairing damaged – body tissue to enable vital chemical reactions to take place. Food is crucial for life because it is the source of energy (ever feel drowsy and lethargic on a fast day?) that drives the chemical reactions that occur in every cell. When consumed, however, food is not in a state suitable for use as an energy source by any cell. The breaking down of larger food particles into molecules small enough to enter body cells is called digestion. The digestive process begins with mouth-watering saliva and ends in the elimination of waste material (accompanied by the *brachah* of "*asher yatzar*" – the most frequently recited *brachah* in our lives) in a dazzling demonstration of food-processing involving specialist machinery (the kidneys, for example, which purify our blood, each contain approximately one million filtration units – each of which comprises a complex array of interconnecting pipework).

A country with no armed forces is vulnerable to attack, and has no means to defend itself. Its survival is at risk. Similarly, from hour to hour, our own survival and good health depends on fending off attacks by disease-producing organisms and attacking invading, harmful cells. Our army is called the lymphatic system, home to the micro-defenders of the immune system. Brave, silent, and devoted, microscopic defenders recognize foreign cells and substances, microbes, bacteria, and viruses, and eliminate them from our bodies using an array of strategies and defense mechanisms. We salute and thank our own Commander-in-Chief, Who supplied us with our personalized armed forces that protect our health.

None of us are the same size that we were at birth, nor do we look the same. Just like tall grass does not grow into trees, so our growth and development is also carefully regulated over our years. Yet another independent wonder, the endocrine system, produces and releases chemical messengers, called hormones, that control and coordinate skeletal growth and vital bodily functions.

Each of these seven systems – skeletal, muscular, nervous, circulatory (heart and blood), respiratory (lungs), digestive, immune, and endocrine (hormones) – is a world of its own in design, planning, and complexity. They all have to work in a coordinated manner for the body to function. If any of these systems malfunction, or is absent, life cannot exist.

Consider: a heart with its valves, chambers, muscular pumping mechanism, electrical-impulse pacemaker, its very own blood supply for nutrients (coronary circulation), veins, and cardiac cycle (rate of heartbeat) needs blood. And blood, the transport system of vital absorbed gases and nutrients required by every single cell, needs the heart to propel it around the thousands of miles of arteries, capillaries, and veins. Blood without a heart might as well sit in a bucket. A heart with no blood cannot function (it needs blood to feed it) and has no purpose. No plumber would install a pump to circulate hot water for the central heating if there is no water. They both need each other. The absence of either spells curtains for the body. One without the other can't work. They must have been created together, at the same time. *Bereishis bara Elokim.*

If a person would be aware of the long series of crucial events that are involved in the formation of a human being – his own very self – then he would see in himself the evidence of G-d. Each individual human being has the power, the ability, and the obligation to see and know. *Mivsari echezeh Eloka* – "From my flesh I see Hashem."

THIRTY-ONE

Ales B'seder? Is Everything Okay?

Mazel tov, mazel tov! The baby has been safely born. The miracles of birth have taken place, each one a cause for wonder and celebration, for the absence of any stage would prevent the safe arrival of this greatest gift. And now, the new baby is hungry.

Several systems need to be present to assuage the immediate needs of the little man. He needs milk to drink, the ability to suckle, the means to swallow, and the guarantee that the precious liquid – his passport to life – will go into his stomach and not his lungs.

Mother has been created with the means to feed her baby. The supply is triggered by the chemical hormone that assists the birth. The milk is the perfect food, containing all the vitamins and nutrients that the growing child requires. It possesses the antibodies that will provide the baby with immunity to illness, its unlimited supply will satisfy the baby and provide him with complete meals for months, and never will he become bored or jaded with the menu.

The baby is born with an inbuilt instinct to suckle. If mother gently puts her finger into her infant's mouth, the baby will suck with gusto. No one has taught him this technique, which involves coordinated muscular activity which is triggered by regular nervous impulses, but without that instinct, the life-giving liquid would be as inaccessible as wine in a sealed bottle, with not a bottle-opener in sight.

Once the milk is safely inside the little mouth, it has to be swallowed. No simple matter. Swallowing starts when the liquid is forced to the back of the throat by the movement of the tongue upward and backward against the palate. The air passage closes, and breathing is temporarily interrupted. Receptors in the throat send messages through the nervous system to the brain, which in turn fires off an impulse to the palate to rise, and for the epiglottis (a large leaf-shaped piece of cartilage lying on top of the larynx) to cover the opening of the wind-pipe. Once the precious liquid has safely arrived at its pre-determined destination, the digestion process can begin.

Here is an example of a multi-faceted operation on which life depends, in which there is no time to learn the skills, where every facet has to work perfectly, every time. Every detail has to be perfect from the beginning, in each generation. Any coordinated system on which life depends could never have developed. It has to be perfect from the start. That is knowledge of a Creator – *yedias Hashem*.

Another function that life is dependent on, which involves many coordinated systems all working efficiently and ceaselessly while asleep or awake, knowingly and unknowingly, is breathing. If you've ever felt the desperation of this function being even slightly compromised (*it was so hot in there you could hardly breathe!*), you know how vital it is to our survival. In the same way that in a subway station, the packed train thunders in, screeches to a stop, doors clang open, streams of passengers disembark, hundreds of passengers squeeze on, doors clang shut and off shoots the train with a rattle of rails – so the breathing mechanism enables all our millions of cells to eliminate the harmful carbon dioxide that has been produced, and welcome the oxygen that they all require to function.

So now you know. Just breathe. But how exactly? How do you ensure that air, with its life-giving oxygen, is drawn into your two lungs, and how will you effect the gas exchange – regularly, automatically, and efficiently? The problem is that there are no muscles in the lungs. Not a single one. So how could the lungs inflate – draw air in, and deflate – expel air? The answer is that the mechanism of breathing is powered by a wonderful system, operated outside the chest. At the base of the chest (thoracic cavity) lies a dome-shaped sheet of muscle – the diaphragm. Muscles force the dome-shaped diaphragm downward, flattening the dome. The ribs are swung outward and upward. The chest cavity has now expanded, vertically and laterally. Simultaneously, the breast-bone moves forward slightly so that the chest cavity is expanded front-to-back. All these movements create a negative pressure – a suction force – inside the chest, resulting in the elasticated lung walls being pulled outward, drawing air in. Breathing out is achieved by reversing the process. A remarkable feature is that the diaphragm, whose downward movement creates the partial vacuum that in turn draws air into the lungs, is actually perforated in three places. This is to allow the food pipe and the two main blood arteries, that lead to and from the heart, access to the lower part of the body. The seal around those three pipes must be perfect; otherwise, the downward pull of the diaphragm would achieve nothing. Try inflating a tire with a break in the seal between the nozzle of the air pipe and the tire valve. In the case of a tire, it would be a deflating experience; in the case of a human being, *oy vey*.

How does the gas exchange work? If you place your finger beneath your Adam's apple (larynx), you will feel your wind-pipe (trachea). It is a straight pipe, about twelve centimeters long, and it reaches into your chest. It then splits into two short tubes, one to each lung, called bronchi. Within each lung, the bronchi split into numerous branches, like an upside-down tree. They divide and subdivide into tiny air passages. Each narrow air-pipe leads to a bunch of tiny sacs, gathered grape-like around its stem. These tiny air sacs give the lungs their spongy texture and appearance; they are the railroad stations in which the oxygen passengers embark and the carbon dioxide passengers disembark. Everyone possesses some three hundred million air sacs, and each air sac is surrounded by a network of capillaries. The capillaries are separated from the air sacs by a thin membrane covered in fluids. This is where the exchange takes place.

The seeming simplicity of the process described is as deceptive as describing blood as red liquid! In fact, the process involves chemistry, atmospheric pressure differentials, and advanced biology – think of a brilliantly designed railroad station. The air arrives on time, like a train, sixteen times a minute (more frequently if you have exercised). On each occasion, the platform is crowded. Silently, millions of carbon dioxide passengers jump on the train for their journey to the atmosphere. And millions of healthy red oxygen passengers hop onto an ever-moving escalator that will transport them around the body. The lungs are your own travel center, containing three hundred million stations, with a train arriving at every station – every four seconds!

Switch off your conscious mind – fall asleep and you do not need to worry. A respirator center in your brain will continue activating the breathing process. It will monitor oxygen and carbon dioxide levels in the blood, and should it detect a build-up of carbon dioxide (after exercise), it will instruct the respiratory system to work at a faster rate, or breathe more deeply.

The system comes with refinements. Breathing is possible through the nose – vital should the mouth be engaged in eating – and in the same way as the trachea is comprised of rigid rings of cartilage that cannot contract (vital for an open airway), so the nose has a bony ridge which holds it in a fixed position. The nose never closes! In addition, as air passes through the nose, it is warmed, filtered, and moistened.

Our breathing apparatus is like the most advanced transport-system imaginable. Trains need engines; engines need fuel, tracks, timetables, signals, coordination, electric, and diesel power. The absence of any crucial factor – add stations and platforms to the menu – will result in stoppage of the whole system. Our breathing needs lungs, a windpipe, muscles, an integrated transport-system linking every cell to the gas exchange, electrical monitoring back-up system, heating, filtering, mechanics, electricians, and chemists. The absence of one single component will cause a cessation of the whole. It either works completely or it doesn't work at all. Our lives depend on it from the first moment after birth until 120 years. There is no time, no chance for development. It must have been perfect from the very beginning. Indeed, *G-d formed man out of dust of the ground and breathed into his nostrils the breath of life* (*Bereishis* 2:7); man thus became a living creature.

Now take a deep breath and with enormous gratitude say the following, "*Al kol neshimah u'neshimah...tzarich l'kaleis l'Hakadosh Baruch Hu* – Praise Hashem for every breath" (*Bereishis Rabbah* 14:1).

THIRTY-TWO

A Glimpse at Yourself

On Purim, the happiest day of the year, the head of the household sits in benevolent mode at his perch at his long dining room table. The spirited, festive meal is in full swing. If he himself has imbibed the requisite volume of alcohol, he will notice little. Which is probably the best situation to be in, given the gradual demolition of his elegant salon as the meal progresses. If, however, he is stony sober, he will scrutinize each visitor with a practiced eye. When a clown-like figure staggers toward him with an unsteady gait, arms outstretched, he knows with absolute certainty that the less-than-welcome visitor has imbibed a high volume of alcohol. How does he know? The irregular zigzagging steps, arms flailing for support, are a giveaway. Why can a sober man walk in a straight line, without support, but a drunken sailor cannot?

Life as we know it depends on us having a sense of balance, connected to a conscious brain. One without the other sends the man collapsing in a heap. The ability to maintain a sense of balance is sufficiently important to merit its own daily *brachah*, *Hameichin mitzadei gaver* – "Who forms man's footsteps." Without balance, no one could walk. We would all be like babies in their pre-walking stage. How would you leave your home? How would you *have* a home? Who could build it if no one had a sense of balance? You would take a brick in your hand and topple forward, pulled toward the ground by the force of gravity. *A chassan* and *kallah* could not stand under the *chuppah*; no marriage, no families. The end of the world! So how does balance work?

A bricklayer uses a spirit-level to ensure that the wall is totally level. A spirit-level is a sealed glass tube partially filled with a liquid, containing an air bubble, whose position reveals the level of horizontal-ness. The Master Craftsman placed organs of מאזנים (balance) just above the אזנים (inner ear). Connected to the fluid-filled cochlea (the organ concerned with the perception and transmission of sound to the brain), lie three tiny semi-circular canals. Each one is about 15mm long, is U-shaped, and is set at right angles to its two other partners. These three angles, each one set at a different plane, can be visualized by looking at the corner of the room, at ceiling level, where the two walls, set at right angles, meet the ceiling at a lateral plane.

Each tiny tube, resembling a spirit-level, is filled with fluid, each with a swelling at one end. Inserted into this swelling is a sense-organ (the cupula), which is perched on top of tiny hairs. As you move, the canals inside your head move also. However, the fluid inside the canals tends to lag behind the movement of its enclosing canals, and the tiny difference of pressure on the cupula makes it tug on the little hairs holding it up, sending nerve signals to the brain. The brain analyzes these signals and interprets them as movement.

The positioning of the three canals at different angles ensures that any movement, in any direction, will be detected; and the necessary instructions will be sent to accommodate the move. If you spin round and round, and suddenly stop, the fluids in the canals continue moving for a while (like water in a bucket swinging when the bucket suddenly stops), telling the brain that you are still spinning. However, the rest of your body is transmitting impulses that the body is stationary, creating contradictory impulses that the brain interprets as the room spinning. Sometimes, when we move rapidly through all three planes of direction, switching from angular-linear to vertical motion (when experiencing air turbulence or a rough sea), nerve impulses pass from the balance mechanism to the vomiting center in the brain – and please pass the brown bag!

Stability is also maintained by the eyes, which, by looking at fixed objects on the skyline or the sides of buildings, keep us aware of true horizontal and vertical planes, which explains the difficulty of maintaining balance in the dark. Not for nothing is the *brachah* thanking Hashem for the ability to stand said at first light, and not at night.

In addition, when you stand to attention and lean forward, you can feel the extra pressure on the front of your feet. Receptors in your feet are shouting (nerve-impulses), "stand straight – don't fall!" Similarly, when you lean forward, you will feel tension in the muscles at the back of your leg. Those muscles have special receptors which are stimulated when stretched, sending urgent messages to the head office pleading for immediate remedial action to prevent falling.

Without all the organs of balance, we could not function. Man was not created to be a crawling worm, but a walking, striding, running, jumping, climbing, carrying two-legged moving machine. Without the ability to walk, man could not defend himself, plant crops, collect food, build shelter, wear clothes, or travel; we would remain at our baby-state of defenselessness and immobility. There is no time to develop all the equipment which every human is blessed with. Two legs pre-suppose a balance mechanism. One without the other has no use or value. Everything was there from the very start.

Walk straight – walk with equilibrium and with poise; dance with joy and with perfect balance with the wonderful machinery designed and provided by our loving Creator.

If we are told in *Iyov* (19:26), *Mivsari echezeh Eloka* – "From my body I see Hashem," then the machinery through which we see deserves its own study to appreciate the wisdom, refinement, and knowledge of the Designer and Manufacturer. To state that the eye is a brilliant camera would be an injustice to the eye. Consider. When light passes through the aperture at the front of the eye (the pupil) and through the transparent lens (do you know of any other part of your body that is transparent? How do you manufacture transparent skin?), it is focused onto the back of the eye (the retina). In this area, covering less than a square inch, lie minute machines, approximately 150,000 to each square millimeter, shaped like rods. Each rod is a distinct machine, connected with a nerve fiber to the brain. Each tiny rod contains a chemical substance called rhodopsin, or "visual purple." When the minutest amount of light (the twinkle of a distant star – a candle at 350 feet) strikes the rod, it causes some of the visual purple molecules to break down, or be bleached. This chemical reaction in turn generates a tiny wisp of electricity – a few millionths of a volt – far too little to tickle a mosquito. This electricity feeds into the straw-shaped optic nerve, and is transmitted to the brain at about 300 miles an hour. The brain interprets the signals flooding in and hands down its verdict. The sight is then sent to the memory bank to be filed away, never forgotten. The visual purple is then re-synthesized, ready for action once again. The whole process takes about two-thousandths of a second.

In addition to the more than 120 million rods that react to light, color vision, with its varied wavelengths, is detected by seven million cones, concentrated in one small area of the retina. They, too, have bleachable pigments which react to light waves of different colors. Like an artist mixing paints on a palette, our brain blends the electrical signals to make scores of different hues.

In order to reduce the number of electrical signals – 130 million separate messages arriving simultaneously is a lot to cope with (imagine each one a visitor arriving at your house!) – an ingenious arrangement combines many signals, enhancing the image and eliminating blurring.

Look with your super cameras at your friend's eyes. Notice how they nestle snugly in a bony cavity, protected and guarded, cushioned with fatty tissue. See how the iris self-regulates according to the amount of light. Switch off the light and switch it on – watch his iris adjust automatically. Observe how the outer layer of the eye is made of tough non-elastic protective tissue, sufficiently strong to withstand the outward force of the fluid inside the eye (vitreous humor), maintaining the spherical shape of the eye, vital for good vision.

Note that each person is gifted with two eyes, each working independently, but together providing perfect three-dimensional vision. Try holding your fingers apart, and joining them together with just one eye open, and you will see the benefit. The two eyes work in unison with perfect muscle coordination, automatically. Six separate muscles, anchored to the skull, allow you to move your eyes sideways, up and down, and all around. The muscle that is attached to the top of the eye, the superior oblique muscle, runs through a pulley to allow it to operate smoothly and freely. One of the refinements of the muscular action is that you can observe a moving object (think of tennis), and a reflex action ensures that you follow the path of the object without conscious effort.

The external part of the eye is protected by eyebrows, eyelids, and eyelashes. Each eyebrow is a bony ridge covered with thickened folds of skin. It shields the eye from sunlight, helps to protect it from blows, and disperses perspiration and rain, directing them to the side of the face. Our precious nose which we faithfully follow, blocks any blows heading in the eye's direction. Painful it may be, but infinitely better than an injured eye.

Drivers of cars will know the hazards of inefficient windshield wipers, or lack of windshield washing fluid. Imagine ill-fitting wiper-blades spreading mud and grime evenly over the surface of the windshield. Worse still – imagine having to sneeze while traveling fast in the pouring rain with spray obscuring your vision, and overtaking a truck while closing your eyes for a couple of panic-filled seconds. Help!

Now appreciate the wonders of a blink. The surface of the eye must be kept moist to prevent it from drying up. Above our eyes are tiny reservoirs containing sodium chloride and sodium bicarbonate, together with lysozyme – an enzyme that destroys bacteria. The wondrous reservoirs are never depleted, never freeze, and spread their cleansing anti-bacterial liquid over the eye once every five seconds (12,960 times a day) automatically. The muscular action that controls blinking is so efficient and so well coordinated that the length of time that the eyelids actually cover the pupil (the aperture through which light passes) is so infinitesimal that it barely registers in the brain and does not disturb the sense of sight at all.

Together with the tears, comes a guttering system at the base of the eyes which empties into the nasal ducts. Eyelids are a perfect fit – when not descending in a blink of an eyelid, they fold away silently and invisibly at the top of the eye, awaiting the next command. An automatic reflex drops the eyelids in the face of excessive glare or an approaching danger.

Every single component of our precious eyes – transparent lens, 130 million rods and cones, the optic nerve carrying those millions of messages, the vitreous humor that gives the eyeball its shape, the muscles that move the eyes in a coordinated fashion, the ligaments that keep the lens suspended in its strategic position, the bony protectors, the eyelashes that curve upward and downward to avoid impending sight, the chemical factories that produce tears, the plumbing system that delivers the fluid and removes the excess, the whizz muscles that power the blink, and more and more, is vital to the ability to see. Without sight we could not function. As in all irreducibly complex organs, every component has to be present, working efficiently, for it to work at all and in order to perform its minimum function. Life as we know it depends on it. In order to work at all, all the components must have been present from the very beginning. Thank You, Hashem, for creating it in its entirety, from the very beginning. *Baruch Atah Hashem…pokei'ach ivrim.*

THIRTY-THREE

Observations of an Observant Jew

There are so many things we take for granted that attest to the wisdom of a Creator. Here is a small sampling:

- Everyone likes eggs, valuable sources of protein. Mix with onions for a favorite Shabbos food, enjoy scrambled, soft boiled, hard boiled, sunny side up, or raw – perfect for *chazzanim*. How was it hatched from the mother hen? If the shell is too hard, baby chick could not exit. If too soft, it would scramble on exit. The thickness has to be perfect from the very beginning.

And the shape! A light bulb, modeled after the shape of an egg, is not much thicker than this page. Yet, it withstands your strong grip when inserted into the socket. The shape is perfectly designed to withstand pressure by deflecting force in all directions. You can try (do not tell your mother, and certainly not your wife) and you will succeed in balancing a table on four vertical eggs. Imitation is the sincerest form of flattery, and millions of light bulbs attest to the formidable strength and perfect shape of the egg – the only shape that would survive birth.

It has to be perfect to be born. For there to be millions of chickens – and all birds – means that their egg birth-capsules have been perfect from the beginning. Otherwise, chicken number one could not have been born. Question: which came first – the chicken or the egg? Answer: the very first chicken, hatching the perfectly shaped egg.

- Our very own, most humble of limbs – please cover them up, wash them regularly – two healthy feet. Each one is a technical masterpiece. If the egg diffuses the pressure of birth, our feet are masters of bearing weight. Just like an arched shape is utilized to support roads, bridges, and dams, so each foot is constructed in an arch shape with the main points of support the heel, the base of our big toe, and base of our little toe. Have a look at your wet footprint in the bathroom and see the evidence.

Each foot contains twenty-six bones (one quarter of the total bones in your body), 107 ligaments, and nineteen muscles. In a standing position, the weight of the body locks the bones of the foot together; the foot is now a solid arch, giving posture and stability. When you walk and run, the bones unlock and instantly become a flexible active spring to propel each step. Without toes, balance, poise, and walking would be problematic in the extreme.

Shock-absorbers in the heel cushion the jarring impact of each downward step. Brisk-walk is 100 steps a minute. Your foot is hitting the cement with a 180-pound jolt millions of times in a lifetime. Without the specially designed thick, cushioned heel, our feet would break into pieces just by walking, which involves tightening and relaxing muscles, maintaining balance, flexing the toes, locking and unlocking the bones, automatic cushioning of blows. There, from the beginning, distributed free at birth, we see our Divine Designer. *Baruch Atah Hashem… hameichin mitzadei gaver.*

• Out of sight, out of mind. Faithful servant; multiple tool; invaluable for speech, digestion, taste, and hygiene: our very own tongue. Extend your tongue and clamp it lightly between your teeth. Now try to speak. In the course of one sentence, the tongue deftly darts from place to place, clings to the roof of the mouth (say "*lamed*"), rolls behind the teeth (say "*tes*"), and lies inactive (say "*vav*"). Consider the subtle difference of tongue position when saying "SSS" and "ZZZ."

After each intake of food, your tongue cannot keep still. Darting here and there, keeping the mouth clear of debris, more efficient than any toothpick, broom, or vacuum. Throughout the entire process, the tongue is busy distributing the food inside the mouth, moving from side to side, in and out, maneuvering the food for chewing, shaping it into the right size for swallowing. Watch people eating (without them noticing!), and see how their tongue extends and curls upward to receive the food and deliver it safely into the mouth cavity, which is invaluable for swallowing, packed with taste buds and brilliant in secreting saliva, which moistens, softens, and begins to digest the food. Food mixed with liquid washes over the taste buds, producing chemical reactions, which trigger electrical impulses that whizz to the brain, which interprets the message to taste, and locks away the information in your memory bank, remembered forever.

Faithful servant that it is, artfully dodging the sharp knife-like teeth, vital to our existence, pure muscles with no bone, constantly active, chemical – electrical – liquid producer extraordinaire; if we cannot manage without it, it must have been there from the beginning, for babies cannot swallow without it. Thank You, Hashem, for a great and valuable gift; our very own exclusive *lashon hatov*.

- Two areas of our body grow constantly. Hair and nails. They both have to be trimmed to allow us to function in comfort. Imagine if your hair and nails were equipped with nerve endings. Why should they not be – the other side of your fingers are packed with heat and pain receivers. Brushing your hair, getting a haircut, cutting your nails would be an unbearable agony. But they have no nerve endings. Painless. Similarly, teeth have to be regularly cleaned and brushed. Imagine them with nerve endings and pain receivers. Agony! They have none. The Designer knows what needs cutting and brushing and cleaning, and created them accordingly. From the beginning.

- Were you able to tie your shoelaces this morning? Turn the pages of a siddur? Open the lid of a glass jar? Make a scrambled egg by holding the egg, cracking it on the side of the glass, and pouring the contents into a frying pan? Untie your *tefillin* and tie them on your arm, and wrap them together again? Then thank your Creator for your thumb. The thumb is a virtuoso. It moves laterally, in a different plane to the other four fingers, and thus allows us to grip. The thumb enables us to perform some 45 percent of the hand's work. A hand without a thumb is like a pair of pliers with one jaw missing. Try sewing a button on your shirt or fastening a button without a thumb. Virtually impossible. I tried grasping the pen that is writing these words without use of a thumb. I couldn't.

Hands without a thumb are not hands. The thumb moves in a different direction, and must have done so from the very beginning. Take a look at your two thumbs and see evidence of a Creator.

- Eat the toughest meat (a note to new husbands) and swallow it without a care. The powerful gastric juices in your stomach will break it down, and eventually digest it. The strong acidic fluid in the stomach, apart from its digestive powers, contributes to defense against invaders by killing many microbes in the food. Question: if the hydrochloric acid is so powerful that it can dissolve the toughest of meat, why does it not dissolve the stomach? Answer: the stomach is equipped with mucus surface-cells that form a barrier that prevents the digestion of the stomach walls.

Which came first – the hydrochloric acid, or the thick mucus wall? Acid without mucus will destroy the stomach. Ouch. Mucus without acid has no purpose. Your fingers do not produce mucus! One without the other cannot be. They must have been there together, from the very beginning. *Bereishis bara Elokim.*

- Nothing demonstrates intelligent design more than valves. A valve is a device for controlling the flow of liquid or gas through a pipe or duct. Every central-heating system contains valves that ensure that the water heated in the boiler flows in the correct direction. Our bodies contain valves. To prevent backflow of blood, the heart has valves. Valves open and close in response to pressure changes as the heart contracts and relaxes. Efficient working of the valves is vital to life.

To ensure safe passage of blood around the body, and to maintain correct blood pressure, our blood distribution system contains many valves. When you stand, the pressure pushing blood up the veins is barely sufficient to overcome the force of gravity pulling it back down. Valves prevent that from happening, prevent any backflow, and ensure that blood moves in one direction only – toward the heart. When you eat, a valve at the entrance to the stomach allows only the amount of food that the stomach can comfortably handle to enter. Without this valve, highly acidic gastric juices from the stomach would leak upward and attack the delicate membrane of the food pipe. Valves regulate the passage of waste water in exiting the body. They regulate the passage of blood throughout the body. They allow the passage of blood from the main heart-pump safely around the body.

Valves do not create themselves. Valves without liquid have no function. The digestive system, the heart, arteries, and veins cannot function without valves. One requires the other, and one without the other cannot work. Valves must have been present (designed, manufactured, and installed) from the very beginning for the very first person to survive.

- In the differing role of genders, men are the instructors, guides, protectors, providers, leaders, and inspirers. Women, equal but different – *eizer k'negdo* – have the role of bearing children, nurturing, soothing, nursing, caring, and homemaking. Therefore, we understand why men are generally taller, larger, have greater physical strength, deeper voices that bespeak authority, and – vital for differentiating genders at night – are bearers of beards that convey signs of age and wisdom. Women, who want to be cared for and protected, who rejoice in providing for their families and being involved in nurturing children, retain their softer, child-like voices. Each gender's physiology is perfectly matched to its role.

- Although our ears receive sound waves and discern speech and our eyes can detect body language (slouch, smile, frown, disinterest, and the full variety of moods), we do not have the ability to read thoughts or transmit thoughts. Imagine the last person you want to see in the world stands in front of you. "Nice to see you," you say, untruthfully. He will not know your true thoughts. What a blessing.

- There is no existential benefit in controlling the passage of waste from our bodies. Members of the animal world are all the picture of health, and leave their droppings wherever they please. But humans are bestowed with a feeling of dignity and self-respect, so the Creator gave us the muscular capability to control ourselves – even at night – and maintain that refinement that makes us human.

- Fruit, vegetables, and flowers, in their multitude of colors, fragrances, tastes, and textures have been created to delight mankind, secure in the knowledge that humans have the sophisticated machinery necessary to discern color, detect and differentiate between tastes and fragrances. So, which came first – the beautiful array of colors and scents, or man's ability to receive and appreciate them? One without the other has no logic and no purpose. *Mah rabu ma'asecha Hashem, kulam b'chachmah asisa.*

THIRTY-FOUR
The Accuracy of Our Transmission

Imagine yourself at a bar mitzvah. The young man – celebrity of the hour – with his new hat perched proudly, if precariously, at the prescribed angle, stands in front of the open *sefer Torah* in shul ready to read his prepared *parshah*. Beside him, brimming with pride, stands his father. Hovering behind him stands his teacher, whispering, "Remember – loud and slow…"

With a quavering voice, the show begins. All goes well, nervousness subsides, until little lad makes a reading mistake. Voices call out, correcting him. He reads again, nervous now, and repeats the mistake. The voices call out again, louder. Mother stands up, alarmed. What's happening to her dear boy? Why can't they leave him alone – don't they know how hard he has prepared, how difficult it is…have pity. But relentlessly, without remorse, the voices will continue until the poor child reads the word correctly.

What a harrowing scene. Whatever happened to not embarrassing someone in public, to the Jewish characteristic of mercy? The boy is so young and it's only one word after all – what harm is there in just letting it go? The answer is: *Toras emes*. The Torah is true, every word, every letter; nothing may be changed, added, or subtracted, and that precious principle overrides everything.

You shall not add to the word that I command you, nor shall you subtract from it – to observe the commandments of Hashem, your G-d, that I command you (*Devarim* 4:2). Anyone who has been involved, either personally or communally, in the commissioning of a new *sefer Torah* will know the painstaking research that precedes the choice of scribe. Why the fuss – what's the problem, every *sefer Torah* is identical, so just go ahead and ask anyone! The answer underscores the accuracy of our Torah transmission. A new *sefer Torah* costs tens of thousands of dollars. Add to that the ceremony that accompanies its inauguration, the celebratory dinner, the silver appurtenances, and the price is doubled. A fortune of money, yet if one single letter of the *sefer Torah* is missing, or extra, or wrong, the entire scroll is disqualified and cannot be used.

There are people who earn their living checking *sifrei Torah*, letter by letter, to guarantee accuracy. In our age of computers, every new *sefer Torah* will be checked, every column scanned to ensure the absence of human error.

The Rambam, in his Thirteen Principles of Faith, declares on behalf of the totality of the Jewish Nation, "*I believe with perfect faith that the entire Torah now in our hands, is the same one that was given to Moshe our Teacher, peace be upon him!*"

That principle of faith is bolstered by the great detail of the body of laws that pertain to the writing of a *sefer Torah*. The *Shulchan Aruch* devotes twenty-one sections (*Yoreh De'ah* Sec. 270-291) containing hundreds of details governing the shape, structure, and spacing of each letter. Whereas some people might think that the Torah transmission consisted of folklore and legend passed from generation to generation around the campfire, nothing could be further from the truth. The Torah we hold in our hands every time we read from it in public is accompanied by a collective declaration, *This is the Torah that Moshe placed before the Children of Israel, upon the command of Hashem, through Moshe's hand.* Indeed, there does not exist, anywhere in the world, any historical document of greater accuracy than the Torah. Protected by inviolable laws and ring-fenced by immutable legislation, we can be absolutely secure in the knowledge that not a single letter of the Torah has been altered since it was first given to Moshe.

During the summer months, and in some communities just between Pesach and Shavuos, a tractate of *Mishnayos* entitled *Pirkei Avos* – "Ethics of the Fathers" – is recited. The six chapters begin with a mishnah that traces the chain of transmission of the totality of Torah, both written and oral. *Moshe received the Torah from Sinai and transmitted it to Joshua; Joshua to the Elders; the Elders to the Prophets; and the Prophets transmitted it to the Men of the Great Assembly.* The reason the Mishnah chooses the Tractate of Aggadic teaching to present the chain of transmission is in order to demonstrate that every piece of learning, even that which would be considered sage advice or quotable quotes, all emanate from the Torah. The whole spectrum of our knowledge, incorporating every aspect of human endeavor, is contained in the Torah.

The accuracy of transmission is not limited to the written Torah, but also to the Oral Law – that vast compendium of detail, practical application, amplification and explanation, without which, clear comprehension of the written Torah is impossible. The written Torah alludes to its oral companion – *These are the decrees, laws and teachings (*Toros*) that Hashem gave, between Himself and the Children of Israel, at Mount Sinai, through Moshe* (*Vayikra* 26:46). The word "*Toros*" is in the plural because it refers to the two Torahs, the written and the oral. This verse emphasizes that both were given at Sinai (Rashi quoting the Sifra).

The Oral Law allows us to read the Torah accurately for, as is known, the Torah contains no vowels or punctuation. It tells us the details, application, extent, and limitation of every single mitzvah. It can be convincingly demonstrated that not one single mitzvah could be observed accurately and correctly without the accompaniment of the Oral Law. For example, the mitzvah of circumcision gives no clear indication on which area of anatomy the surgery should take place. When the Torah forbids "all manner of work" on Shabbos, no explanation is given that defines "work." That would be a serious omission, particularly since working on Shabbos is a capital crime. The manner in which animals are dispatched to render them edible by humans (*shechitah*) is not mentioned specifically. There are no details. Perhaps we should swing the cow around our heads by its tail and fling it at a brick wall? We need an oral explanation.

The absolute accuracy and faithfulness of the oral transmission can be demonstrated by observing Jewish practice. The Torah was given in the year 2448 – some 3,330 years ago, at the time of writing. For the last two thousand years Jews have been scattered around the world; more often than not as refugees, persecuted and harassed. Segments of our nation have been isolated from mainstream Jewish population centers and tradition (i.e. the Jews of Yemen) for two and a half millennia. Yet, every Jewish male wears *tefillin* that are black and square, and contain the same four passages, word for word, from the Torah. Not a single Jew in the world has triangular *tefillin*, pink in color, containing *zemiros*. Everyone on Sukkos shakes the same collection of four species. No one has daffodils and a bunch of roses. Every kosher animal is *shechted* throughout the world by means of a single cut with the sharpest of blades through the trachea and esophagus. Every home in every land has a *mezuzah* on the right-hand doorpost on entry, on which is written precisely the identical two Biblical passages. Everyone observes Shabbos on the same day, refrains from the same thirty-nine categories of creative work, and recites the same Biblical passage when making Kiddush over a cup of wine. Dietary laws are identically observed in every kitchen (although customs vary as to which color dish-cloths designate meat and milk) and every Jewish marriage follows the same format under the *chuppah* (although musical styles are as varied as the flags at the UN).

It is often said that if a medieval scholar would sit down in a contemporary classroom, he would not understand a word. Not the language, not the concepts, not the knowledge, and not the mindset. In contrast, if Rashi would walk into a yeshivah, he would pull out a Gemara, understand every word, converse with every *bachur*, join them for Minchah, *lein* from the Torah, talk in learning with the *roshei yeshivah*, and feel absolutely at home. And the same would apply to all our great leaders, all the way back to Moshe Rabbeinu. Nothing has changed.

Apart from the documented unbroken chain of transmission through the generations, the accuracy of the Written and Oral Law is further underscored by the tremendous stress which is laid on study. Every Jewish man is enjoined to know the Torah, and devote as much time as possible to its study. Study of Torah is our primary occupation, our pastime, our hobby, our vocation, and life-long occupation. *Sefer Yehoshua* begins with a Divine instruction – to learn Torah: *This Book of the Torah shall not depart from your mouth, rather you should contemplate it day and night...* (*Yehoshua* 1:8) and the last book of Tanach ends with the same message: *Remember the Torah of Moshe My servant, which I commanded him at Horev (Sinai) for all of Israel, its decrees and its statutes* (*Malachi* 3:22).

The Torah that we study is a Torah of life. It is studied, analyzed, discussed, argued over, debated, and dissected. It is lived and it is breathed. Whoever studies it very quickly becomes aware of its vast complexity, its endless and fully coordinated massive body of detail, in which every letter of the Torah has to integrate with the others. In just the same way that every neuron in the brain is connected with every other, making the brain more complex in its connection system than all the telephone exchanges in existence, so does the Torah share that same level of complexity and coordination. *Ta'amu u'reu*, taste it and see the Divine design on every page of Talmud.

Further corroboration of the Torah's Divine authorship and accurate transmission is to be found in the world of codes, in which names, places, events, names of *sefarim* written, are clearly encoded in equidistant numbers or letters. The statistical probability for such a multitude of examples to have happened by chance is zero!

Probably the greatest attestation of the Torah's veracity is the honesty of the teachers and transmitters of that Torah. Beginning with Moshe, we have, as described, a man who never imagined himself to be – or never harbored an ambition to be – leader of the Jewish Nation. We read how Moshe was given no *protektzia* and no privilege. Together with his brother Aharon and sister Miriam, he was held up to the closest scrutiny in every detail of his conduct – with every slight misdemeanor revealed and punished. Moshe and Aharon were denied entry into the Land of Israel, Miriam was excluded from the camp for seven days. The very first, as well as the last communication from Hashem to Moshe were words that went against Moshe's own personal wishes.

The first: *Do not come any closer... Take your shoes off your feet...* (Shemos 3:5).

The last: *This is the land regarding which I made an oath to Avraham, Yitzchak, and Yaakov, saying, "I will give it to your descendants." I have let you see it with your own eyes, but you will not cross* (the river) *to enter it* (Devarim 34:4).

The greatest possible approbation was given to Moshe by Hashem, ...*Not so is my servant Moshe; in My entire house he is the trusted one* (*Bamidbar* 12:7). Trusted means reliable, truthful, honest, genuine, unambitious, and loyal. Moshe admitted the truth when he forgot a halachah (*Vayikra* 10:20). He was the most self-effacing of men; yet when accused by his cousin Korach of self-aggrandizement and selecting himself as leader – which, given Moshe's qualities of absolute integrity, was an accusation of the greatest treachery – Moshe demanded from Hashem the most powerful reaffirmation of his Divinely-bestowed appointment. *...This shall demonstrate to you that G-d sent me to do all these deeds, and I did not make up anything myself*, and, as we know, his request that Korach and his followers should be swallowed up by the ground was fulfilled.

You have to meet an absolutely honest man – someone who you know will never lie; never cheat you; is never devious, conniving or cunning; always reliable and conscientious – to know who Moshe Rabbeinu was. And that quality of trust and honesty – *ne'emanus* – is the hallmark of every Jewish leader, and has been so since Moshe Rabbeinu. It is the characteristic of Hashem – *Kel Melech ne'eman*; it is the underlying theme of every prophecy and every promise; indeed, of every word of the Torah. The Hebrew word for truth is אמת – א is the first letter, מ is the middle, and ת is the last letter. And that tells you everything.

Our sages say, *Teach your tongue to say I don't know* (*Brachos* 4a). The Mishnah in *Avos* (5:9) enumerates the seven characteristics of a learned person. The final point is *about something he has not heard, he says "I have not heard"; and he acknowledges the truth.* Our Torah leaders are unlike politicians – they are not voted into office – and they gain their reputation from their standard of learning, and the sterling qualities of their character. Men of truth, representatives of the Torah of Truth, do not shy away from admitting a mistake, or error of judgment. Their agenda is not self-aggrandizement, but pursuit of truth in the service of Hashem. If reliability is what you are seeking, you will find it in the Torah.

In presenting the facts which underpin our belief system, our *emunah*, we have shown the national experiences of the whole people at the Exodus, and seven weeks later at the Revelation at Mount Sinai. The Torah is written in the experiential present, which means that those who received the Torah lived the events described. *Hashem said to Moshe: This is what you should say to the Children of Israel – You have seen that I have spoken to you from Heaven…* (*Shemos* 20:19). Everyone saw everything.

In contrast, the subscribers to the Theory of Evolution (a Divinely directed word: "evil-לשון" with לשון pronounced in a *chassidishe* manner) speak of events of hundreds and millions of years ago; witnessed by no one; speculative, wishful thinking, desperate to avoid ascribing the wonders of creation to a Creator. In the faithful tradition of *harotzeh l'shaker yarchik eiduso*, those who wish to deceive, they present testimony of long, long ago; three hundred million years ago, a brave tadpole climbed out of the lake and altruistically decided to grow legs… Well, you can claim anything from eons past without worry of refutation, but consider:

- If evolution is factual, it should be a continuous process; but we do not see it anywhere. We humans are not growing wings, pianists do not develop an extra finger, and Jewish babies (or their fathers) have not developed an extra stomach to accommodate cholent. Worldwide, there is complete absence of any species showing evidence of evolving with new organs.

- If we are developed from lower species, there should be millions of fossils of all the intermediate stages – apart from all the living hybrids of half-ape, half-humans. After 150 years of digging around the world, there is complete absence of *any* fossil evidence of *any* intermediate species.

- Go to the zoo, and ask the monkeys in the cage why they stubbornly refuse to evolve. Why did every living ape, monkey, chimpanzee, and every member of your wider family refuse to evolve further?

- Every mutation has its limits. Despite centuries of effort, no blue rose or black tulip has ever been produced.

We Jewish people have a tradition, unbroken and privileged, to enjoy the greatest guarantees of accuracy and veracity, satisfying every criteria of accuracy and honesty; that 130 generations ago, our forebears saw and heard Hashem communicate to His people. We are the direct descendants of the witnesses of that event, our line has remained pure, the story has not changed, not a letter altered; and in that communication, Hashem told us, and we all heard it, that He exists, and that He created the world. One hundred and thirty generations is not a long time. Some of us are fortunate to experience seven generations in one lifetime; great-grandfather, grandfather, father, self, son, grandson and great-grandson, 130 pictures around the room, and you are back at Mount Sinai. Nothing has changed. Our story is one of *yediah* – empirical evidence, sensory perception, knowledge of Hashem, and witness by the whole nation. And the opposing forces scream their defiance, unremitting in their ridicule, bombastic in their denial – but offering no cogent disproof or counter-evidence. All they have to offer is a mythological fairytale of three hundred million years ago with no evidence, which is statistically impossible.

We are the ones with knowledge, a rock-solid trustworthy tradition of direct communication from the Creator. The opposition, whose liberal lifestyle depends on their idolatrous ideology, are the ones with a fanatical, almost religious belief in the impossible. But when a person is driven by desire and passion, with a wish to be free from any form of restraint or discipline, then man is given the freedom of choice, *harotzeh l'ta'eis yavo v'yateh*.

Ashreinu mah tov chelkeinu, the Jewish People are the most fortunate; we have solid knowledge and national experiences that are underpinned with truthfulness, trustworthiness, and honesty. We are the one nation in the world, still strong, vibrant, and viable, who fulfill the command of *v'yadatem hayom*.

The mission of each individual is to be acquainted with that knowledge, live with it, incorporate it into the very essence of his being, and faithfully transmit it to future generations.

וידעת היום והשבת אל לבבך כי ה' הוא האלקים בשמים ממעל ועל הארץ מתחת אין עוד – *You are to know this day and take to your heart that Hashem is the only G-d in Heaven above and on the earth below, there is none other* (*Devarim* 4:39).

תם ונשלם שבח לקל בורא עולם